D0699502

Class in the
Twentieth Century

Class in the Twentieth Century

Edited by

Arthur Marwick
Professor of History
The Open University

St. Martin's Press
New York

First published in the United States of America in 1986

Printed in GREAT BRITAIN

ISBN 0–312–14254–4
Library of Congress Catalog Card Number 86–17888

Contents

Acknowledgements

This book contains the historical contributions made to an interdisciplinary research seminar on class organised at the Open University in the early 1980s. For the basic financing which made the project possible, I should like to thank the Open University Research Committee and also Professor Norman Gowar, the then Pro-Vice Chancellor (Planning). For a very substantial award which made possible the three-year researches of Angi Rutter, I should like to thank the Leverhulme Foundation; a period of subsequent work by Angi Rutter was financed by the German Historical Institute, to whom also my warm thanks. Some of the research for my own chapter on the upper class was undertaken at the Hoover Institution, Stanford University, California and I should like to thank that body for the Visiting Scholarship they awarded me in 1984–85. Grateful acknowledgement is also due to the British Council for financing a long trip by Margaret Smales to Prague and Bratislava in 1980–81 and a two-month visit to Prague in 1982.

Academic colleagues from the History and Literature Departments and from other areas of the University participated vigorously in the seminars and I should like to offer very sincere thanks to all who did participate, and particularly to Graham Martin, Clive Emsley, Bernard Waites, Tony Aldgate, Bob Owens and Nick Furbank. A fairly late version of my own chapter was delivered to a Hoover Institution Seminar and I should like to thank the colleagues there who commented critically and constructively upon it. Professors James Joll and Bill Wallace were examiners for Maggie Smales' thesis, and their comments have also proved very helpful.

Karen Hazell carried out all of the secretarial work in regard to the seminar and a very great deal of it in regard to my chapters. I offer her my most sincere thanks; I would also like to thank Sabine Phillips who typed the final versions of my chapters.

CHAPTER ONE

Introduction: The Pragmatic Historical Approach

History is not an easy subject. In a most extreme form, it is affected by a problem common to most intellectual disciplines, but particularly to those concerned with human behaviour, human institutions and human values. The problem is the conflict between the very proper wish to impose order and sense upon the data, offering explanations which are persuasive and logically consistent, and the fact that the data are themselves almost without limit, difficult to interpret and full of confusions and contradictions. Subjected to a violent attack for his attempts to bring a Marxist analysis to bear upon developments in seventeenth-century English society, the distinguished British historian Christopher Hill referred to the fundamental distinction 'between those who try to make sense of history and those who see nothing in it but the play of the contingent and the unforeseen, who think everything is so complicated that no general statements can safely be made, who are so busy making qualifications that they forget that anything actually happened.'[1]

'Class' is a much-used, perhaps fundamental, concept in historical discourse. Discussion of it throws up in virulent form the disagreements between those who wish to apply a body of theory and thus 'make sense of history', and those who, while usually going beyond 'the play of the contingent and the unforeseen' essentially remain agnostic about the value in historical study of anything more than the most limited and specific theoretical concepts. The difference is often seen as being essentially a political one (clearly there is likely to be a correlation between having a Marxist view of history and

1

having left-wing political views), but it may be that a more crucial factor is the psychology, or 'mental set' of the individual: to some the refinement of theory, the excitement of developing a science which might provide deep truths about the organisation of society, is irresistible; to others theory seems often simply to obscure and distort those truths which can be ascertained by empirical methodology.

'Class', in one of its most important usages, lies at the heart of a body of important and influential sociological theory dating back, in some aspects at least, to the later eighteenth century. Every textbook dealing with class has sections on Karl Marx (1818–83) and Max Weber (1864–1920).[2] A number of simple, but none the less very important, points have to be made: the views of Marx and of Weber frequently differ, the views of both have been greatly elaborated and modified in the twentieth century—of particular relevance to this book are the highly sophisticated formulations of Lukács, Althusser, Poulantzas and Habermas, of the Marxist Structuralists and Post-Structuralists, and of the Birmingham School of Cultural Studies;[3] to take up an intellectual position on class derived from Marx or Weber or both is not to be necessarily committed to a left-wing or any other political standpoint—Ralf Dahrendorf, author of *Class and Class Conflict in Industrial Society*,[4] stands to the right-of-centre in German politics. The basic points central to this body of theory can be summarised as follows:

1. With the development of industrialisation societies have become divided between two fundamental *classes*, capitalists and labour, though, in response to the complexities of modern society, 'intermediate' or 'middle' classes have also emerged.
2. It is a fundamental interest of the capitalist class to exploit labour, and it is a fundamental interest of labour to resist this exploitation, and perhaps even to seek to overthrow or supersede the capitalist class; thus the essential relationship between these two fundamental classes is that of *conflict*.
3. Modern classes are an inevitable concomitant of industrial capitalism and a person's 'objective' class position is determined by his relationship to the capitalist

mode of production, or (more simply) by his position in the market.

4. A distinction may be made between a person's 'class' (his objective relationship to the capitalist economy) and his *status*, that is to say his position in the hierarchy of prestige (for example, by one, rather extreme, argument, a professor, entirely dependent on his salary, might be seen as belonging to the same class as a factory worker, though obviously occupying a different status).

5. Individuals and groups are not necessarily conscious of their true class position and their true class interests; if they are and if, for example, they form a particular labour or socialist party to press these interests, then they are 'class-conscious'.

6. Those aiming explicitly at the supersession of capitalism expect that system to be succeeded by 'socialism' and are themselves 'socialists'.

It would be foolish for any scholar, historical or literary, engaging with any aspect of class, to ignore this body of theory (which, of course, I have grossly condensed and simplified). It should, however, be remembered that the tradition emanating essentially from Marx does not monopolise western scholarship. The French sociologist Durkheim took a rather different view of industrial society, seeing classes as being integrated in a kind of mutual dependency, rather than being in an inevitable state of conflict. There is a rather important French school of empirical writing on the subject of class which offers persuasive portrayals of industrial society without laying any stress on the significance of class conflict.[5] A more thorough-going alternative formulation to that summarised above would argue that, whatever significance class may or may not have had in the nineteenth century, it has in the twentieth (the chronological context for this book) become an irrelevant term, so that society, rather than being divided into two, or perhaps three, classes, is better thought of as presenting a continuum, perhaps consisting of a continuous gradation of different 'status groups'.[6] To dwell on class, and class distinctions, in this view is to betray a warped mind.[7] My alternative formulation is a rather different one. It is that an abundance of evidence for both the nineteenth and twentieth centuries indicates that industrial societies do divide up into broad aggregates of individuals (to use Weber's cautious and useful phrase) distinguished from each other by inequalities in wealth, income, power, authority, prestige, freedom, life-styles and life chances (to use another of Weber's useful phrases), including prospects of mobility into a different 'aggregate of individuals'. These aggregates seem to me well described by the term 'class'. However, the use of the term 'class' does not automatically imply that these aggregates must be in conflict with each other, nor does it imply any universal explanation as to how these aggregates came into being in the first place, such as, for example, the Marxist explanation that a class is determined by its relationship to the dominant mode of production; or Anthony Giddens's more sophisticated recent formulation that the upper class is characterised by 'property in production', the middle class by 'education'.[8] For most of the remainder of this Introduction I shall expound this pragmatic approach to class.

Self-styled pragmatists must always be on the alert for the criticism that they are just as embroiled in theory or assumptions as the next person, but that they are blind to their own prejudices and preconceptions. In a sense, there is no answer to the accusation; and the critics, anyway, usually would not accept anything short of total capitulation. But the pragmatists' counter-attack (in effect at least as hard to rebut) will usually be that far from adhering to a scientifically validated body of theory, the Marxist or other theoretician is merely acting out a drama of faith, little different in principle from that of, say, the committed Christian. Let me at any rate try to identify what I take to be my own assumptions. I assume that the desk in front of me is indeed a desk, that what I perceive is indeed reality, and that there are not somehow deeper structures which I cannot perceive; more to the point, I believe that historical documents, in all their variety, are indeed documents and that, for all that they are fragmentary and very far from simple to read, they will, if treated with the evaluative and critical skills of the professional historian, and weighed up one against the other, and one against the accumulation of other documents, yield up concrete evidence about the past.[9] In studying, say, Magna Carta, historians know that they must interpret its clauses within the context of the ideas and assumptions of a particular social group in early thirteenth-century England. Thus historians know very well that in writing their own histories they are bound to be victims of their own social context; the pragmatic historian strives at all times to try to surmount the restrictions of his own time and place, but knows that he will never totally succeed. He knows that the preoccupations and modes of expression of historians have changed as contemporary preoccupations have changed. However, in recognising his own fallibility, his own thraldom to his own culture, the pragmatic historian will feel bound to insist that what is sauce for him must also be sauce for Marx. Marx was the product of a particular nineteenth-century environment; much of what he wrote was an eminently reasonable extrapolation from the circumstances of his time. The pragmatic historian of today would not wish to claim either the prodigious intellect or prodigious energy of Marx, but would claim the advantage over Marx of having both absorbed the many important insights which Marx had to offer to scholarship, and seen the way in which many of Marx's most important predictions were simply falsified by actual events. I freely recognise the immense sophistication of much twentieth-century Marxist writing (not, however, that of Lenin); yet *either*, in my view, the theory (whatever the refinements and adjustments) still stands and remains, what it always was, an act of visionary faith unsubstantiated by the evidence; *or* the modifications have been so great that the theory no longer stands, and the practitioners are really pragmatists claiming only to be Marxist because that is thought by them to keep them securely on the side of the angels when it comes to matters of contemporary political debate.

It is a commonplace, and something of a dead horse,[10] that historians cannot do without concepts and generalisations. From this it is sometimes argued that they are stranded midway in a quagmire of unformulated theory and that security is only to be found on the further shore of fully developed Marxism.[11] Alternatively, it is argued that if the historian does foreswear grand-scale theorising then he has sunk into the bottomless pit of nominalism whose denizens 'are so busy making qualifications that they forget that anything actually happened'. Let me therefore make it clear that, as a pragmatist, I believe in theor*ies*, but not in one all-embracing theory; I welcome the use of micro-theory and, indeed, macro-theory, but reject meta-theory. In my own earlier work on war and social change,[12] I derived immense help from the disaster studies of social scientists, from theories of military participation and of shared values, and I recognise also the utility of the very precise models provided (in economics) by, for example, location theory, and the theory of the product cycle.[13] The test of any theory in science, in technology, in the arts, and in the social sciences is, 'Does it work?'; not so much, in our case, 'Does it have predictive value?', but 'Does it have analytical value?' Does it help in that problem-solving which is an essential part of all intellectual activity? Does it contribute to the answering of genuine and precisely delimited questions? I deeply resent the arrogant assertion that the historian who seeks out his evidence (often a very taxing task in itself), who applies to it the complex techniques of source criticism, is somehow a fuddy-duddy positivist studying only the external aspect of events while the true reality can only be perceived by those who have an insight into the alleged inner structure of social processes. I reject the affectation of these initiates that they have assembled some great scientific corpus of knowledge. Because, in fact, when you test out their meta-theory, whenever in fact it is possible to test it, you usually find that it doesn't work. How many articles, how many books, have we read about why there was no revolution in Britain at the end of the First World War?[14] If you forget the meta-theory, there was never any good reason in the first place to believe that there was any likelihood of a revolution at that time. As an historian, I am not concerned with the unfolding of an alleged historical process, with the replacement of one so-called social order by another, with the superstition that there is an alternative condition of socialism waiting to succeed to capitalism. I am concerned with the solving of medium-range problems. Why did Britain alone of western countries produce a genuine Labour Party? How far do English novels represent the distinctive shaping and colouring of British class structure? Why does there appear to be no consolidated upper class on, say, the British or French model, in inter-war Czechoslovakia? What was the impact of the

Second World War on social structure in the United States? Did West Germany after the Second World War come anywhere near to achieving a society without class distinctions? Have Britain's current economic problems been caused by an excessive obsession with class?

I should add to all this that I believe that very many historians have written of class in a sloppy way, generally, without much self-awareness, employing an insecure mix of impressionism and Marxism. A special value of this book is that it is deliberately self-conscious in its usages of 'class', while engaging with actual topics in history and literature, rather than simply being yet another history of a concept. I am asserting the right to use the word 'class' to connote these society-wide aggregations of individuals, separated by an interrelated series of inequalities, to which I have already referred, without its being automatically assumed that I see these classes as having the characteristics which Marx attributed to them. Marx, after all, did not invent the word 'class', and no sociological theory has a monopoly on how one should use that word. It is, however, best to recognise that the phrase 'class-consciousness' has come to have a special technical meaning which is inextricably bound up with Marxist theory. 'Class-consciousness' entails a clear recognition on the part of an individual or individuals within a class of their own special class interests, of the way in which these interests are in conflict with those of other classes, and a determination to share in the struggle on behalf of their own class (through, say, forming a Labour Party, or taking part in strikes). To me it is evident that individuals can be aware of belonging to a class which is distinctly different from other classes, without subscribing to the notion of conflict or taking up an activist stance. Thus, I refer to 'class awareness'; this seems to me the simplest and most straightforward term, though I recognise that R.S. Neale has had much the same thing in mind in speaking of 'class perception', while, on the other hand, Anthony Giddens has something altogether different in mind when he speaks of 'class awareness'. Giddens writes:

An initial distinction can be drawn between 'class awareness' and 'class consciousness'. We may say that, in so far as class is a structurated

7

phenomenon, there will tend to exist a common awareness and acceptance of similar attitudes and beliefs, linked to a common style of life, among the members of the class. 'Class awareness', as I use the term here, does *not* involve a recognition that these attitudes and beliefs signify a particular class affiliation, or the recognition that there exist other classes, characterised by different attitudes, beliefs, and styles of life: 'class consciousness', by contrast, as I shall use the notion, does imply both of these. The difference between class awareness and class consciousness is a fundamental one, because class awareness may take the form of *a denial of the existence or reality of classes.*[15]

In admiration for the elegance and symmetry of Dr Giddens' writings, I am second to none. This passage, however, comes close to perverse mystification: it projects upon a class the *assumption* that a class must have distinctive 'attitudes and beliefs', and it uses 'class awareness' to mean *not* being aware of belonging to a particular class.

The point has often been put to me that because there always are these possibilities of confusion I should leave the term 'class' to the Marxists, myself using the ugly sociological metaphor of 'social stratification'. But the fact is, one simply cannot get anywhere in historical writing without using such phrases as 'the middle class', 'upper-class accents', 'working-class housing', etc. Since one has to use the word, without necessarily in any way using it in a Marxist sense, why substitute the ugly jargon of 'social stratification' for the plain straightforward 'class'?—particularly since, as I have twice shown, it is perfectly easy to offer a clear and comprehensible definition of what it is one means by a class.

I have defended my use of class, and I have criticised some historians for some looseness in theirs. Let me now, therefore, describe what I believe to be the proper historical approach to the subject of class. Classes, as would be widely agreed by most non-Marxist historians, and probably by many Marxist ones, came into full being under the impact of industrialisation; however, the older social structure of estates, 'stations' or orders, had been transformed over a far longer period of time as a result of the growth of commerce and manufacture. Elements of nineteenth-century class structure were already apparent in the seventeenth century; elements of pre-industrial social structure continued into the nineteenth and twentieth centuries, for historical legacies frequently override industrial imperatives. It follows from what I said about the need to deal with medium-range problems that I believe it more important to establish the particular forms taken by class in different societies than to establish some general model of class roughly applicable to all industrial societies. Thus the first task, as I see it, is to establish the *historical context* which determines the particular shape which class and class relationships will take in a particular society.[16]

Among the elements which go to make up the historical context of class I would single out geography, history and tradition (including educational and other cultural institutions); levels of industrialisation and the nature of industrial relations; and ideologies and modes of expression (to include the actual vocabulary available to give expression to perceived social differences). In regard to geography, for example, the very vastness and variousness of the United States, the geographical sectionalism, the provincialism of much of the Middle West, and the absence of one undisputed metropolitan centre, have all affected the shaping of class in the United States. France and America each have their (rather different) revolutionary traditions; Britain has had a continuous tradition of aristocracy, revered in a way in which no aristocracy has been revered in the United States. The significance of the British public schools has been much commented on; but scarcely less significance attaches to the prestigious American private schools and Ivy League colleges. A vital key to one crucial aspect of class formation and class attitudes in Britain is that industrialisation came so early and so massively that a large, entrenched and well-organised working class was becoming firmly established by the 1850s and 1860s. In the more sporadically industrialised France of the nineteenth century there was scope for the rise of the great capitalist barons, such as Neuflizé and de Wendel. An ideology of mobility and maintenance of purchasing power militated against the growth of working-class awareness in the United States; the elaborate detailed vocabulary of the French *Codes* (*artisan, petit commerçant, moyen industriel*, etc.) also tended to cut across the formation of self-aware social classes. It was in Britain and France, almost simultaneously, in the late eighteenth century that the word 'class' appeared in widespread usage.[17]

A construction of the historical context (derived, of course, from the critical study of the enormous available range of traditional documentary, visual and statistical source material) does not in itself convey a picture of social structure. It is merely indicative of the particular forms social structure will be likely to take. The next stage is to establish how social structure is perceived from within the society studied itself to see whether, an *a priori* determination to use the label 'class' apart, there is any evidence within the society for envisaging it as being made up of several classes. This involves the systematic study of a series of *images of class* organised according to the provenance of the documents studied. The idea is not the simplistic one that if one reads enough accounts by the people of the period and society one is studying of how they see themselves and others, a clear and reliable picture of class structure will automatically emerge; nor is it the naive one that no social fact can be regarded as true unless it is to be found in a document. Of course, the views expressed in the documents frequently conflict: the point is to dig for the *unwitting testimony*, not the overt opinions, but the assumptions about class and social distinctions which are so much a commonplace to the people themselves that they are not even aware of what they might be revealing to an historian with the requisite skills.[18] The objective is to build up a series of mappings of overall class structure, and of individual classes within the class structure, filtering out the clearly eccentric data, and superimposing one mapping upon the other so that eventually an overall 'map'[19] emerges which, while not the creation of any single perception or group of perceptions, would be broadly recognisable to individuals of the period and society studied as a valid reconstruction of the class structure of their society. Essentially the questions one is attempting to answer are: 'Do contemporary sources recognise the existence of those broad aggregates, not underpinned by overt legal sanctions, which we can describe as "classes", and, do they, indeed, also so refer to them?' And, 'What overall mapping or configuration do they suggest for these "classes"?' Because the people of a particular society see their class structure in a particular way that does not, of course, establish with certainty that that is how the class structure really is. But we shall certainly have made substantial progress in our investigation.

First of the sets of images (or perceptions) to be examined are those I label *academic and polemical*. I start with these because academics (social scientists in particular), politicians and writers of polemical treatises have a vested, even professional, interest in studying the topic of social structure. They will no doubt have the usual range of ulterior motives, but at least they will have given attention to the subject. I run academic and polemical together to make the point that no privileged position is being given to professional works of social science; they are primary sources like any other, to be valued as much for their unwitting, as for their witting testimony. One might expect a Marxist sociologist and a liberal democratic sociologist to give wildly different accounts, just as one would expect a left-wing politician to differ sharply from a right-wing one. In fact this is the sort of naive assumption that only those unused to the handling of historical evidence would make. Where there is a distinctive peasant class, as in France or Czechoslovakia in the inter-war years, both the Marxist and the liberal democratic sociologist will recognise this. Though the Conservative politician in Britain may argue that the separate classes should unite together for the national good, while the Labour politician will indict the gross inequalities between the different social classes, the basic assumptions about the actual nature of British society, as a society in which in fact different classes do exist, turn out to be remarkably similar. Thus one is looking for the common denominators, the shared assumptions. Out of these one will be able to build quite a sophisticated, well-articulated model of society as perceived by these professionally interested groups.

Next one turns to *official images*. How is class portrayed in census reports, official investigations, legislation? As is now widely known,[20] the categories of government censuses bear little relationship to class divisions as popularly understood and as represented in the other types of source. Thus the direct perception of social structure of the census will usually simply be filtered out. On the other hand, legislation is enormously revealing of, for instance, the different way in which manual workers and white-collar workers are treated in such matters as social insurance. Using the bold outlines established by the study of academic and polemical images one can start filling in details and qualifications derived from the official evidence.

From there one moves to the most fascinating source of all, what I have variously dessribed as *private, unofficial, and popular images*, but what might, following Maggie Smales, be conveniently termed *informal images*.[21] Here we get closest to what people without any professional or official axe to grind think about social structure as a whole, and their own position in it. Here one consults letters, diaries, autobiographies, reminiscences, interviews, oral evidence. Perhaps the profusion of evidence would be too chaotic, but already one has controls: the *shape* one might expect class to take given the nature of the historical context, and the *outlines* already established and qualified by the previous two sets of images. The informal images, many simply being filtered out, again fill up and qualify the mappings already established.

Finally, there are *media images*. From novels, from plays, from films, from photographs, from cartoons, from advertisements, from the many artefacts of popular culture, one can derive further insights into assumptions about the nature of social structure. Of course, with the possible exception of certain novels, such media will be almost exclusively in the hands of the rich and powerful. Frequently there will be an overt political message, fostering the notion of social integration and harmony, for instance. But again it is possible to look behind such witting testimony to the deeper assumptions, those points about society which everyone at the time regarded as commonplace, but which are so valuable to the historian. These points come out particularly strongly when one compares films from different cultures: one then becomes aware, for instance, that there are social indicators in American films that simply could not exist in British or French films, and so on.[22] I have set out the four sets of images in mechanical series; often it is true with films or with creative literature that they suggest new thoughts on, offer new clues to, class structure, thoughts and clues which then have to be traced out again in the more traditional types of source material.

From all of this, then, one builds up a picture of class and class relationships which would, in general, have made sense to most people living in the society being studied. One at least has labels for the different classes which ring truer than such inventions as 'bourgeoisie' and 'proletariat'. Now is the time, in the third section of our investigation, to check out the picture we have received, the labels we have garnered, against the hard (mainly, but not exclusively, statistical) evidence of inequality in wealth, income, power, authority, prestige, life-styles and life chances. If, for example, from our four sets of images there emerges a clear sense of the existence of a separate and coherent upper class, one can then check to see whether or not there does seem to exist such a class exercising disproportionate control over cabinet office, senior civil service positions, and top posts in finance and industry. One can correlate the lines of demarcation between classes presented by our images with the established facts of income distribution. One can look at the geography of housing to see whether it corresponds with the notion of a division into certain specific social classes. The final upshot should be a rounded, and distinctive, model of class structure firmly related to the particular historical context of the particular society studied, and in which so called 'subjective' evidence is firmly integrated with so-called 'objective' evidence.

But that is not enough. The whole purpose of getting an accurate, distinctive, model of class (as opposed to a model simply derived from meta-theory) is to enable one to handle medium-range questions. What is the significance of this model of class so painstakingly assembled? How does class, as a source of inequality, compare, say, with race, or with sex? What influence does class structure have on voting patterns; what influence on economic or political performance? It becomes possible to work out answers to these questions because we have a different and distinctive model of class for each society studied in which the *differences* stand out. Comparative evaluation is therefore possible.

The question to ask of the pragmatic historical approach is: Does it work? Does it yield results? Three chapters which follow eschew *a priori* preconceptions, while endeavouring always to be precise about what is being studied and how. Chapter 2, arguing that an upper class, though in each case a slightly different one, exists in each of the three major western societies, suggests a possible answer to the puzzles about the actual size and boundaries of the upper class, by offering the notion of an 'extended upper class', which, it is maintained, fits both the realities of the exercise of power and possession of wealth in the three countries, and the perception of the upper class held in these three countries. Chapter 3 offers the first ever full analysis of the social structure of the inter-war Czech Lands, freed both from the popular myths of the time and the system-building of Czechoslovakia's subsequent rulers. If Chapter 4, on the German Federal Republic since 1945, has rather more secondary literature to contend with, so also does it have to try to clear up many confusions and contradictions. It denies the myth of classlessness and suggests a basis for defining the social structure of West Germany along lines that would make sense to the inhabitants of the Federal Republic themselves.

Notes

1. *Time Literary Supplement*, 7 November 1975.
2. The literature is enormous but can be followed up in the bibliographies of the books noted here (I confine myself to recent publications): Philip Abrams, *Historial Sociology* (1982); Leslie Benson, *Proletarians and Parties* (1978); Peter Calvert, *The Concept of Class: An Historical Introduction* (1982); Anthony Giddens, *The Class Structure of the Advanced Societies* (new edition, 1980); Anthony Giddens and David Hale (eds.), *Classes, Power and Conflict* (1982); Pauline Hunt, *Gender and Class Consciousness* (1980); Vincent Jeffries and H. Edward Ransford, *Social Stratification: A Multiple Hierarchy Approach* (1980); R.S. Neale, *History and Class: Essential Readings in Theory and Interpretation* (1983); Frank Parkin, *Marxism and Class Theory: A Bourgeois Critique* (1979); Erik Olin Wright, *Class, Crisis, and the State* (1978); Z. A. Jordan (ed.), *Karl Marx: Economy, Class and Social Revolution* (1971).
3. Georg Lukàcs, *History and Class Consciousness* (new German edition 1967, English translation 1971); Louis Althusser, *For Marx* (1969); Nicos Poulantzas, *Political Power and Social Classes* (first French edition 1970, English translation, 1973); Jürgen Habermas, *Communication and the Evolution of Society* (English translation 1979); Julius Sennat, *Habermas and Marxism* (1979); C.R. Badcock, *Lévi-Strauss: Structuralism and Sociological Theory* (1975); Roland Barthes, *The Empire of Signs* (1970, English translation 1983); Susan Sontag

(ed.), *A Barthes Reader* (1982); Stuart Hall (ed.), *Culture, Media and Language* (1980); John Clarke, Chas Critcher and Richard Johnson, *Working-Class Culture: Studies in History and Theory* (1979).

4. Ralf Dahrendorf, *Class and Class Conflict in Industrial Society* (1959); see also *Conflict after Class* (1967).

5. Emile Durkheim, *The Division of Labour in Society* (1st French edition 1893, English translation 1933); Maurice Halbwachs, *The Psychology of Social Class* (1959), *Les Classes Sociales* (1942); François Simiand, *Cours d'economie politique* (1929); Pierre Laroque, *Les Classes sociales* (1972); Jean Lhomme, *Le Problème des classes* (1938); Louise-Marie Ferré, *Les Classes sociales dans la France contemporaine* (1934).

6. In the 1950s this approach held sway among certain American sociologists who explicitly stood aside from discussing 'social class', e.g. Gerhard Lenski, 'American Social Classes: Statistical Strata or Social Groups?', *American Journal of Sociology*, vol. 58 (1952), p. 139; A. Reiss, 'Occupation and Social Status', *American Journal of Sociology*, vol. 61 (1955). The famous Kinsey spoke not of 'working-class men', but of 'lower-level males'.

7. In his classic work *Equality* (1932), p. 65, R.H. Tawney noted that 'the word "class" is fraught with unpleasing associations, so that to linger upon it is apt to be interpreted as the symptom of a perverted mind and jaundiced spirit.' Most recently, Peter Calvert, *op.cit.*, p.216 has asked: 'Should we, therefore, abandon the concept of class altogether?' replying: 'The answer is almost certainly yes.' He advocates the elimination of what he terms 'classism'.

8. Giddens, *Class Structure*, p. 107.

9. This belief is expounded and justified in Patrick Gardiner, *The Nature of Historical Explanation* (1952); R.E. Atkinson, *Knowledge and Explanation in History* (1978); Geoffrey Elton, *The Practice of History* (1967); Arthur Marwick, *The Nature of History* (revised edition 1981).

10. The matter was thrashed out in a thorough, not to say painstaking way, in Louis Gottschalk (ed.), *Generalisation and the Writing of History* (1963).

11. Neale, *op.cit.*, p. 274, rubs his hands because he catches me using concepts; but that does not, as he obviously thinks, make me an unwitting Marxist.

12. Arthur Marwick, 'The Impact of the First World War on British Society', *Journal of Contemporary History*, vol. 3, no. 1 (1968), pp. 51–63, *Britain in the Century of Total War* (1968), *War and Social Change in the Twentieth Century: A Comparative Study of Britain, France, Germany, Russia and the USA* (1974), 'Problems and Consequences of Organizing Society for Total War', in N.F. Dreisziger (ed.), *Mobilization for Total War* (1981), pp. 3–21, and 'Total War and Social Change in Great Britain and other European Countries', in *Proceedings of the Tenth Military History Symposium, U.S. Airforce Academy, October 1982* (1984), pp. 130–46.

13. For an application of 'location theory', see Thomas C. Cochran, *The Inner Revolution* (1964), pp. 20–3. For use of 'the product cycle', see

Tony Dickson (ed.), *Scottish Capitalism* (1980), pp. 181–2.

14. See e.g. Walter Kendall. *The Revolutionary Movement in Britain, 1900–1921* (1969); Keith Burgess, *The Challenge of Labour* (1980); James Cronin, *Industrial Conflict in Modern Britain* (1979); James Cronin and Jonathan Schneer, *Social Conflict and the Political Order in Modern Britain* (1982).

15. R.S. Neale, *Class in English History 1680–1850* (1981), pp. 155–92; Anthony Giddens, *Class Structure*, p. 111.

16. See my *Class: Image and Reality in Britain, France and the USA since 1930* (1980); and 'Images of the Working Class', in J.M. Winter (ed.), *Essays in British Labour History'* (1983), pp. 215–31.

17. See Calvert, pp. 58–63.

18. On 'unwitting testimony', see Marwick, *Nature of History*, p. 144.

19. The idea of class as 'map', of course, pre-dates Marx's technical use of the term: in his *A Treatise on the Wealth, Power, and Resources of the British Empire* (1814), pp. 106–7, Patrick Colquhoun presented 'A Map of Society in 1814', consisting of seven 'classes.'

20. Marwick, *Class: Image and Reality*, p. 62; the point had been perceived in a work of popular humour, Jilly Cooper, *Class: A View from Middle England* (1979), p. 15.

21. See Chapter 3, below.

22. See Arthur Marwick, 'Le film *est* la reálité, in *Analectures*, 1, Spring 1983, pp. 34–49.

CHAPTER TWO

The Upper Class in Britain, France and the USA since the First World War

The role of the English public schools, as they emerged in the second half of the nineteenth century ('public' because they drew their pupils from across the country, not just from the immediate locality, but, in fact, expensive and exclusive private boarding schools, inculcating 'muscular Christianity' and traditions of leadership and service to the nation) is proverbial.[1] One famous headmaster at the turn of the century, of whom a pupil said 'he would be an awful bully if he wasn't such a terrible Christian', envisaged his school, where 'the curriculum was primarily classical' as 'turning out well-rounded gentlemen dedicated to public service and unselfishly holding the reins of power in the nation'. This 'headmster' was in fact Rector Endicot Peabody of Groton, an exclusive private boarding school on the East Coast of the United States.[2] British writers on class have tended to concentrate on the British upper class while, perversely, insisting that in so far as this class does not match the classic Marxist model of the ruling bourgeoisie, it is unique and should not be taken as characteristic of western society generally.[3] I shall, on the contrary, argue that the British example is central and instructive, and that in both France (to a greater degree) and the United States (to a lesser degree) there are features which have too often been written off as purely British phenomena. Even in regard to the United States I speak of an upper class, not of an élite or élites. This is not to argue that élite analysis is irrelevant, simply that the existence of an upper class continues to be extremely important. If, as Suzanne Keller puts it, 'For élite recruitment as a whole social class will be a variable rather than a constant element',[4] then upper-class status is a peculiarly important variable, though with slightly different weighting in each of the three countries studied.

Among historians who recognise the existence of an upper class or, often, a 'ruling class' (a phrase I prefer to avoid), there is little agreement as to its size. Gabriel Kolko has identified in America 'a small class, comprising not more than one-tenth of the population, whose interests and style of life mark them off from the rest of American society'; but, 'within this class, a very small élite controls the corporate structure',—'the "sports-car", "country-club", or "Ivy League" set.'[5] For this élite Kolko appears to have in mind a figure of a few thousands, also the kind of figure Michael Useem has pinned on his 'capitalist class'.[6] In the most recent of his series of impressive works on America's 'ruling class' William Domhoff has reiterated his original calculation of 'at most 0.5 per cent'.[7] This perception would coincide with that of Russian Premier Nikita Krushchev: when Averell Harriman invited Krushchev to be precise in identifying the membership of America's alleged ruling capitalist class, Krushchev replied, accurately at least with respect to the individual and the family, 'You're one of them'.[8] Laurence H. Shoup, however, gives a figure of 1–2 per cent.[9] Writing of Britain, John Scott defines the 'core of the business class' as consisting of less than 0.1 per cent of the population.[10] French authorities offer figures ranging from 1–2 per cent to as high as 5 per cent,[11] though French journalist Jean Baumier takes us right down to the other extreme in his admirable *From the 200 Hundred Families to the 200 Hundred Managers*.[12] Statistical calculations have to use the statistics as they exist: unfortunately attempts to pin down major property-holders, or to study the wealthy, do not come up with conclusive answers: indeed, Adeline Daumard, dealing with France, confesses to the impossibility of the task: 'While certain names of the wealth-holders are frequently cited, a serious study cannot be undertaken.'[13] One figure which holds great appeal, perhaps because it combines the positive sense of a class larger than a mere élite or cousinage with a very obvious recognition of highly restricted privilege, is that of 1 per cent: W.D. Rubeinstein has wittily reminded us that 'the wealthiest percentile of the population will invariably number 1 per cent of the total population'.[14] He has also pointed out that, in Britain (and this would also be true of France) the accumulation of massive wealth is 'highly anomalous',[15] something which is rather less true for the United States (a crucial difference, in fact, between the North American and European upper classes); nevertheless, Rubinstein's point holds true that millionaires in themselves do not constitute a social class.

My contention will be that if we look at how the upper class actually appears within the societies studied, and how it actually operates, there is little validity in the concept of a tiny upper class of 0.1 per cent, that even 0.5 per cent remains on the low side, and that rather than there being a distinction between a ruling élite and a substantial 'service' or 'governing' class, there is one 'extended' upper class of, say, 2–3 per cent, which can then be distinguished from what may quite appropriately be termed the upper middle class; indeed I prefer this formulation, even in the American context, to the somewhat mechanistic 'upper-upper, lower-upper' version recently reiterated by Edward Pessen in a valuable article which, drawing on older works, does concur with the 3 per cent figure.[16] This is not to deny that there are separate fractions within the upper class or even, to adopt a spatial metaphor, concentric rings. In Britain the innermost circle is not that of a thousand or so corporate directors, but of much longer-established groups which attract the prestige and define the life-styles which then permeate the other circles of the upper class; in the United States there are 'colonial' and 'old-stock' groups. At any point in time, my argument will be, some fractions of the upper class belong to it as of right, some are socialised into it, some individuals and families actually make voluntary decisions (or certainly are affected by contingency) over whether to accept the socialisation process, or whether to remain determinedly middle-class,[17] but the boundary is there all right, for once inside the upper class the rewards and opportunities are quite disproportionately greater than those available to persons who remain within the middle class. However one must follow Domhoff's magisterial studies in recognising that there is some quantitative difference between the American upper class, and that of Britain and France. His figure of 0.5 per cent 'is based upon the number of students attending independent private schools, the number of listings in past *Social Registers* for several cities, and details interview studies in Kansas City and Boston'.[18] But Domhoff does speak of the assimilation and socialisation of rising executives and of the close interrelationship of experts and 'high level employees' with the original 0.5 per cent in forming a 'power élite':[19] my argument will be that even in America, Americans themselves (as distinct from a tiny minority of social scientists) do not recognise a power élite, or members of it, or behave as if it exists but that they do recognise an upper class, or at least, upper-class individuals and families, and that this upper class is an extended one in the way in which Domhoff himself suggests.

The methodology employed is the three-stage one described in Chapter 1.[20] By examining the historical context I hope to establish the *likelihood* that we would find a form of upper class in each country, the differing forms being related to differences in the historical contexts. Then, by bringing together academic and polemical images, informal and private images, and images drawn from the media and popular culture I hope to show that an upper class is indeed perceived as existing in the three societies and to pin down the features which are seen as characterising these upper classes; I miss out official sources since the upper class is too small to be noticed in them (this is why so many studies based essentially on census material treat society as divided solely into a working class and a middle class). Finally, I endeavour to integrate these perceptions with the 'realities' of the distribution of power, wealth and status. In industrialised societies no upper class is static. This paper focuses on two separate periods, the inter-war years, and the period since the 1950s. Great changes took place throughout society, yet, I shall argue, the three upper classes, though certainly not unaffected, proved remarkably resilient; in many ways, indeed, the American upper class is more sharply in evidence in the later period than in the earlier one. Of course, dissimilarities are almost as important as similarities, above all in regard to the differing contributions of the three upper classes to the general histories of the three societies.

The Historical Context

Britain in the twentieth century had the most obvious formal symbols of a separate upper class; an hereditary peerage unbroken since the Middle Ages, hereditary baronetcies, and a system of knighthoods and other honours which in general marked the achievement of a certain status within the upper sections of British society; furthermore, there was a less formal, but scarcely less well-defined, recognition of which families occupied county or gentry status. Long before the Industrial Revolution families whose wealth derived from national or international commerce had been recruited into the aristocracy or gentry. Industrialisation provided the foundations for new family fortunes, though financiers were consistently better rewarded than industrialists: while the most successful figures from finance, the higher professions, and, also, industry moved upwards in the social hierarchy, there was also a reaction against mere middle-class money-grubbing which served to enhance the status of old-established professions, particularly the Anglican clergy.[21]

Under the pressures of industrialisation, indeed, there was a reorganisation and consolidation of those institutions which could play a crucial role in maintaining and developing an aristocratic, or upper-class, ethos. The Clarendon Commission of 1861–64 gives its name to the nine prestigious schools, Eton, Winchester, Westminster, Charterhouse, St Paul's, Merchant Taylors, Harrow, Rugby and Shrewsbury which, together with perhaps about the same number of other very celebrated public schools, became the educational establishments for those already clearly at the top of society, or else on their way there.[22] With short terms, long vacations, exclusive clubs and sporting activities, the two ancient universities of Oxford and Cambridge well served the function of finishing schools for both the genuine, and the aspiring, aristocracy.

Britain, then, had the forms, trappings and institutions of an aristocratic upper class securely built round a titled system, openly recognised and legally defined. Matters were otherwise in France, where the French Revolution had substituted common citizenship for the legally defined estates of the old

21

regime. Titles had reappeared under the second empire, only to be abolished under the third republic, which nevertheless maintained an honours system of crosses and ribbons as rich as that persisting in Britain. In twentieth-century France many families did indeed claim titles, or at the very least the noble particule, but there was always a touch of insecurity or defensiveness behind such claims. The French ballerina Cleó de Mérode went to some trouble to maintain that her noble-sounding name was authentic: when doubts were expressed by, as she put it, 'one of my friends, the Duke of N' she produced papers to demonstrate not only the genuineness of her connection with the House of Mérode but also that her title was rather better than the Duke's.[23] In France there was no secure aristocratic structure of custom and behaviour into which successful new recruits could be socialised. Instead, the nobility was rather an appendage to a social group or groups which rose partly through the free workings of the mercantile and industrial economy, and partly through the direct patronage of the republican state. Bankers were at least as important as in Britain in forming a privileged social group: as early as 1806 Napoleon had created the 200 Regents of the Bank of France, the basis of the twentieth-century notion of France having a ruling clique of '200 families'. Limited and patchy industrialisation in France provided the opportunity for a handful of monopolists to achieve positions of eminence above that generally achieved by industrialists in Britain: hence such famous families as Schneider, De Wendel and Neuflizé. The French education system was dominated by the state, but fees at the *lycées* (run by the central government) or *collèges* (run by the local authorities) put them beyond the reach of most families, and certain of these secondary schools, particularly those in Paris and the major provincial centres which took boarders, commanded an enviable social prestige. Even after secondary education became free in 1933 there were many other costs associated with education in the *lycées* or *collèges*. At the top of the ladder were the *grandes écoles*, providing entry into the most prestigious and influential jobs, above all those of the higher civil servants (*haut fonctionnaire*) who, in keeping with a continental tradition, had a status above that occupied by its analogue in Britain, and, in effect, automatically formed a kind of nobility.[24] Quite on a level with the *grandes écoles* as a training ground for top civil servants, and with a special social cachet of its own, stood the private, and extremely expensive, School of Political Sciences (the 'Sciences Po.').

Rather different traditions again held sway in the United States. American society, with its own revolutionary and pluralistic history, resisted the prestige and authority so readily granted to those in government and administration in France and, to a lesser degree, in Britain.[25] The anti-aristocratic tradition of the American Revolution was of course strong. When a supporter of William Green, President of the American Federation of Labor, wished to express his bitter contempt for John L. Lewis, Leader of the Congress of Industrial Organisations. The word he twice used in a private letter was 'lord'.[26] In the main east coast centres, commercial, financial and professional families built up their own traditions of exclusiveness, reinforced under the threat of the new wealth created by industrial expansion in the late nineteenth century. In the south, the planter class asserted a social supremacy not so very different from that obtaining in the less industrialised parts of Europe. As a reaction against new threats, the old-stock groups in the 1880s and 1890s either converted old grammar schools, or established new foundations, to create a body of exclusive private schools designed to inculcate their own exclusive ethos. In fact, like the more exclusive public schools in Britain, these schools became institutions for socialising the products of new wealth into this ethos.[27] They included Philips Academy, Andover, Massachusetts (1778, converted into an exclusive upper-class school about 100 years later), Philips Exeter Academy, Exeter, New Hampshire (1783, similarly converted 100 years later), Hill School, Pottstown, Pennsylvania (1851), St Paul's School, Concord, New Hampshire (1856), St Mark's School, Southborough, Massachusetts (1865), Lawrenceville School, Lawrenceville, New Jersey (1883), Groton School, Groton, Massachusetts (1884), Hotchkiss School, Lakeville, Connecticut (1892), Choate School, Wallingford, Connecticut (1896), St George's School, Newport, Rhode Island (1896), Middlesex School, Concord, Massachusetts (1901) and Kent School, Kent, Connecticut (1906).[28] But the 'extensions' of the upper class did not go so far as in Britain. There are a number of reasons for this. The opportunities for accumulating great wealth, open in particular to those already in the upper class, are so great that the financial gap between those already there and those making their way up on salaries and modest investments is much greater than in Europe. In America, there is not the central, prestigious function of government and civil service to bring together wealthy families and merely professional ones.

The geographical vastness and variousness of the United States are important factors, placing difficulties in the way of a truly national dominance for old-stock east coast families, or southern planter gentry, and creating a kind of provincialism in the Middle West, not very different from that which we shall find in a Czechoslovakia cut off from Austria and its great metropolis, Vienna, a provincialism which implies the absence of any true upper class. There are many centres of local influence in the United States and thus great resistances to socialisation into an upper class. France had regional centres, and therefore regional notables; Britain, rather, had provincial centres: but both countries had a famous metropolis, an essential adjunct to the upper-class life.

What language was to hand in the different countries to describe these privileged social groups, products of history, geography, economic development, tradition and education? In France occupations were legally codified in a manner not true of either Britain or America. To be defined by any of the vast majority of these occupational labels (for example, *artisan, commerçant, instituteur*—primary school teacher—*petit industriel*), it is clear, is to be defined as not belonging to any superior social grouping. However, the label *haut fonctionnaire* would place one very high up in society, as might also being included in a *profession libérale*. Other less formal labels of relevance here are *noble, intellectuel* (both implying high status on a national scale), *notable* (which implies local eminence), and *mondain* (belonging to high society). 'Bourgeois' is less straightforward. Quite frequently 'bourgeois' is used, not as a sign of high social status or great economic or political power, but as a social put-down: 'the bourgeois', wrote the sociologist Maurice Halbwachs, is 'a man without distinction'.[29] Where the sense of a clear superiority is being implied, a qualifying adjective is needed as in *grande* or *haute bourgeoisie*.

The notion of 'the gentleman', as we shall see in later essays, plays an important part in images of class in other continental European countries. In Britain the notion was undoubtedly still a potent one at the end of the First World War. Half a century earlier, distinctions were clearly apparent as between an aristocrat, a member of the gentry, and a mere gentleman. But under these pressures to which I have already referred it was coming to be recognised that someone who could be described as 'a gentleman' (whatever exactly that might mean) had more in common with those assuredly at the top of society, than he had with the vast uncultivated mass. There was no rigorous definition of what constituted a gentleman in early twentieth-century Britain. A too manifest preoccupation with earning a living excluded one (unless one had inherited gentility from more fortunate forebears); conspicuous display of leisure time spent on civilised pursuits, and, above all, on 'service'—in the army, in politics, on civic bodies, in the best professions—helped to bring one in. In the end, being a gentleman tended to equate with having been to a good public school.[30] In America, both the labels 'aristocracy' and 'upper class' were in use. So was the label 'gentleman', but with still less precision than in Britain. Gentlemen's clubs were important institutions in all three countries; but peculiar to the United States were such clubs as the Daughters of the American Revolution and the Junior League. The label *clubwoman* becomes an important indicator of high social status. Finally, a few words about accent and linguistic style. It is simply not true that such matters had no significance outside of Britain. In the 1950s Hollywood comedy *Some Like it Hot* (set in the inter-war period) Tony Curtis, in his disguise as an Ivy League gentleman seducing Marilyn Monroe, adopts a distinctive, if somewhat odd, accent. In 1976 a whole issue of the French left-wing journal *La Pensée*, was devoted to the relationship between class and use of language. One contributor speaks of the norm being established by the 'cultivated speakers' who inhabit a particular part of the sixteenth *arrondissement*.[31]

Now some specific points relating respectively to the two periods I have chosen for study. In all three countries the First

World War was ambiguous in its effects. The war experience did, as I have argued at great length elsewhere,[32] have some levelling effects on the older upper class. It also brought some prestige to new elements making their way up into the upper class, while at the same time creating resentment against these elements if they were seen as war profiteers. Thus, as a counterpoise, still more prestige accrued to those older 'gentlemanly' professional groups to which I have already referred. For the more recent period it is important first to consider the thesis of the 'managerial revolution' which was alleged to have had the effect of separating out ownership of capital from management, thus making 'middle-class' managers important in a way that 'upper-class' owners of capital were not.[33] In fact most recent work has shown that nearly always big owners of capital themselves become managers, while successful managers usually seize the opportunity to acquire capital.[34] The second total war again had levelling effects, and in the years following it many new sources of income and prestige become available, particularly with the growth of the mass media.[35]

Britain in the Inter-Wars: Images

This section seeks to establish that in the Britain of the time there was a widespread recognition of the existence of a distinctive privileged class at the top of British society, that while the label 'upper-class' was more readily applied to individuals than to the class as a whole, this none the less is the most acceptable label, and to show where the lower boundary of this class was felt to be. In the 1930s, when the BBC was gingerly discussing the dangerous prospect of mounting a radio series on class, one of the governors, Sir Ian Fraser, in a private letter, vouchsafed a telling image. 'England', he wrote, 'has gained much by having a class of people not compelled to earn their living, who have been able to devote their ability and time to developing our art of government, free institutions, etc.' Other countries, he continued, had suffered from political instability through not having this 'reservoir of persons economically free and accustomed to responsibility from an early age'.[36] The notion of a 'reservoir' is a particularly apt one: each member of the upper class does not necessarily exercise power, but he has, if he so wishes, privileged access to it. Perceptions from below were not quite so clear: trade union leader George Isaacs lumped the 'middle class' in with the 'working class', separating out at the top 'the so-called leisure class'.[37]

The more austere academic sources tended to speak of 'the rich', 'the wealthy' or 'the well-to-do'.[38] A much more romantic imagery is offered in the much-quoted works of popular sociology by C.F.G. Masterman. In *The Condition of England* (1909) Masterman had referred to an upper class of 'Conquerors'; in his overly dramatic *England After the War* (1922) he referred both to 'The Passing of Feudalism' and to 'The Plight of the Middle Class'.[39] His asides are of more value than his assertions: having at length discussed 'the Middle Class' as exclusively inhabitants of the suburbs, he then recognises a rather more influential group, 'an additional Middle Class—the *bourgeoisie* of the Continental Socialist definition'.[40] The journalist and social critic H.W. Nevinson brought the class at the top of society more sharply into focus. To belong to it, first of all, a 'certain scale of property' would be essential, since the customary education at preparatory school and Public School ('there are only about half-a-dozen whose names carry social prestige', Nevinson has already told us[41]) would cost a father more than £2000 in all.

If his income was derived from land, either in town or country (that is, from rent paid him by tenants), so much the better. But a highly successful barrister or physician, or the Head of a college, might enter the social circle, and so on rare occasions might the writer of a popular novel, or the painter of a picture much talked of at the Royal Academy show. . . .

The successful City man, the Company Promoter, or a speculator might also reach the confines of Gentleman. And officers in the Army and Navy were there by nature. So perhaps were the Clergy: at all events, in the country we used to be told that 'The cloth will take you anywhere'.[42]

All of this was in connection with a discussion of the achievements of the popular novelist John Galsworthy, who had recently died.

Galsworthy, Nevinson wrote was: 'Born among the wealthy classes, supplied from boyhood with every comfort and advantage, at a Public School and Oxford, intimately acquainted with horses and dogs, an experienced traveller for sport and pleasure, a welcome guest in Society, handsome, strong, a good athlete, married to a lady of remarkable beauty, charm and intelligence . . .'[43] Edward Garnett, at one time Galsworthy's literary mentor, put it still more precisely: Galsworthy, he says, 'had himself passed through the upper-class mills of the Public School, the University and the Bar'; he 'stands for the best of the upper-class Englishman of his period . . .' He knew 'his own class', Garnett concluded, more thoroughly and intimately than any author of his period.[44] Here, according to two independent sources, we have an actual member of the upper class. What were his objective circumstances? From Devonshire yeoman stock, Galsworthy's grandfather had settled in London in 1833 and made a vast fortune out of London's rapid urban development. Galsworthy's father established his own solicitor's firm in the City of London, and owned several country houses. Galsworthy himself, as Garnett emphasised, became a barrister.

The published letters of another figure prominent in popular literature, Sir Henry Newbolt, show him as being on easy terms with, and indeed part of, the most powerful in the land.[45] Newbolt's career would seem to confirm Nevinson's assertion about the Anglican clergy. Newbolt was born in a palatial vicarage (two main staircases and two subsidiary ones, three large sitting rooms, and three entrances) at Bilston in the Black Country; his mother's father was a banker and a dominant influence in the town of Walsall. After a prep school in Lincolnshire run by his father's old Cambridge tutor, Newbolt went to Clifton (as a day boy). He provides some interesting sentences on the relationship of the public school to this extended upper class which I have postulated:

The boarding-school comes of aristocratic ancestry: it is the attempt to perpetuate the old custom by which well-born boys were sent to lodge with still better-born patrons—knights, noblemen or bishops, upon whom they waited and from whom they learned the arts and exercises of social life. The housemaster of our public schools is often the right man to carry on this tradition, but he is overwhelmed by numbers. The class by which such an education is desired is now far larger, and less wealthy in proportion . . .[46]

J.C.C. Davidson, known to historians as the powerful confidant of Stanley Baldwin in the inner circles of the Conservative Party, clearly saw himself as a member of the topmost class in society, and just as clearly saw that class as extending to the higher ranks of the learned professions, while he sees war profiteers as outsiders trying to force their way in. In a letter to Lord Stamfordham, the King's Secretary (no less!), he wrote, shortly after being elected a Conservative MP in February 1921:

> The first thing that struck me on entering the House of Commons was the high percentage of hard-headed men, mostly on the make, who fill up the ranks of the Unionist Party. The old-fashioned country-gentlemen, and even the higher ranks of the learned professions, are scarcely represented at all. I cannot bring myself to believe that this is a good thing, and I cannot help hoping that the next Parliament will be less full of the modern, and to my mind unscrupulous, characters which are to be found in the present House. . . .[47]

Davidson himself was scarcely an old-fashioned country gentleman. His paternal grandfather had been a small Perthshire farmer who, after emigrating to the Argentine in 1825, became a major landowner there, with a variety of other lucrative investments. Davidson's father, born in 1857, was educated at the Scottish school in Buenos Aires, and subsequently studied medicine at Aberdeen University. He became a lecturer in Ophthalmology and then an ophthalmic surgeon; he also became Head of the British School of Radiology. With his salaries, fees and private income from Argentina, he was able to set up a substantial establishment in Portland Place, London. The young Davidson was sent to prep school. 'With me,' he wrote, in what would seem like parody were it not that this sort of sentence rolls out with complete solemnity over and over again in the autobiographies of the eminent, 'were Oliver Lyttleton (now Lord Chandos), 'Bobbety' Cranborne (now Lord Salisbury), and Duff Cooper (later Lord Norwich).'[48] From prep school, Davidson went to Westminster School, and then on to Pembroke College, Cambridge in 1907 to read law.

The private and informal sources are full of evidence of the distinctive self-image held by those whom I would include in this upper class. Political persuasion is not an especially relevant consideration; meticulous attention to every detail in the breeding of close associates is. J.C.C. Davidson noted that 'Hugh Dalton was the great man in my day at Cambridge, and for the rest of his life whenever he greeted me, he used always to boom out in that horrible voice, "of course, we were at Cambridge together". He was a fourth-year man, very arrogant, and detested by everybody and by no one more than myself.'[49] The detestation may have been retrospective since Dalton became a leading figure in the Labour Party. The rise of the Daltons, incidentally, brings out both the importance of the Church of England connection and, above all, the importance of royalty at the apex of the prestige system. In the 1830s Hugh Dalton's grandfather had been Rector of Milton Keynes. His father, after achieving great theological distinction at Cambridge and then serving as a curate, became first of all tutor to the royal princes, then Canon and Steward of St George's, Windsor. On flights to France soon after the outbreak of the Second World War Dalton made boisterous jokes about how he and the Conservative Robert Boothby were both Etonians, while all the others on the flight were Rugbyans. Earlier, he had made notes on his new private secretary: 'Winchester, Trinity Cambridge (double first history), FO . . .'.[50] Similarly Captain Harry Crookshank, Eton and Oxford, Foreign Office, Conservative MP at the age of 31, Secretary for Mines, 1935–39, noted in his diary that the Chief Inspector of Factories was 'an Eton and Magdalen man'. Crookshank, who was always having 'bother with the servants' and finally decided to sack the lot, quoted favourably the homily of Lord Trenchard, formerly Chief of the Air Staff and before that a cavalry officer, in which he described a gentleman as 'one who looks after his men first'. Crookshank's social philosophy was simply: 'people can't all have the same chance: what we want is to see everybody has *a* chance. You can't train a carthorse to win the Derby.'[51] The upper class, in their own image of themselves, were thoroughbreds.

In the later 1930s Hugh Dalton moved freely in and out of the foreign policy discussions held among dissident Conservative politicians and civil servants.[52] In the 1920s Robert Boothby was on close terms with John Strachey, who described himself as an 'upper-class Socialist'.[53] Sir Stafford Cripps, described by J.T. Murphy, an engineering worker and former member of the Communist Party, as 'a very likable person, though a trifle conscious of his old school tie', became notorious in the press in the 1930s as 'the Red Squire'.[54] Yet, when in the early days of the war he found himself in lonely isolation as Britain's ambassador to Stalin's Moscow, it was not to his socialist cronies he turned, but to his fellow barrister, the Conservative MP, Sir Walter Monkton: 'Does your mind ever play like mine with the old days when we battled in the Courts? They seem very remote but that [sic] are happy memories to me and a great comfort and resource.'[55]

There was, I have suggested, a traditional inner ring to the upper class. To an aristocrat at that centre, such as Lord Londonderry, Neville Chamberlain, Conservative Prime Minister in the late 1930s, could be referred to as 'a Birmingham tradesman'. But Chamberlain, as Captain Margesson, the Conservative Whip put it, had been to the 'usual' [sic] preparatory school and public school, and that public school was Rugby. Chamberlain had his full measure of upper-class old-boy sentimentality.[56] (His half-brother, Austen, had, in the 1920s, projected a more thoroughly aristocratic image—he was the statesman 'who always played the game, and always lost'—but the money came from the same source, industrial Birmingham.) What images do we have of those who do fall outside the upper class? Eric Blair (George Orwell), as is well known, was at great pains to stress his 'lower-upper-middle-class' position.[57] He does seem a very good example of someone on the fringes of the upper class who might, had he made different choices, or had immediate circumstances been slightly different, have established a definite place within it. The family had aristocratic connections, but a great grandfather had squandered his considerable fortune. Orwell's grandfather was a Church of England vicar, and his father, one of twelve children, had for economy's sake to be educated at home, and thus achieved no higher appointment than that of an official in the Opium Department of the Government of India, from which he retired to England with a pension of £480.10 per annum, a solid middle-class salary in the Edwardian period, but far short of what was needed for an upper-class life-style. Orwell won a scholarship which enabled him to go to a prep school for half the annual fees (£90 instead of £180), and subsequently won a scholarship to Eton. Had he cashed in on Eton, won say a further scholarship to university, Orwell might, exploiting his Etonian connections, have established himself in the upper class. As it was, he did not have a particularly distinguished school career and ended up in a Burmese government post not dissimilar to that occupied by his father. (Someone who was already securely established in the upper class would not, of course, have been under any necessity to do well at Eton.)

Daughter of a scholarship boy, who passed up a chance of going to Oxford, but who became a professor of philosophy, Mary Agnes Hamilton spent a life-time on the fringes of high politics and, apparently, on the fringes of the upper class. She went from a board secondary school in Glasgow to Newnham College Cambridge where, her revealing comment is, 'To one who knew nothing of boarding schools, the college smelt like one.'[58] John Boyd Orr, son of a Scottish businessman, became one of the world's greatest nutrition experts and, eventually, a peer. But he remained resolutely apart from the upper class, as this comment indicates:

The top civil servants, like the ministers, are drawn from the public schools and from Oxford or Cambridge. . . . Their education means they are indoctrinated with the ideas of the ruling class giving them a nostalgia for the past and they resent change.[59]

With J.B. Priestley, son of a schoolteacher and adult education lecturer, we move further into the middle class. As Priestley has noted, at the age of sixteen he had either to leave school or work for a university scholarship. He left school, but eventually reached Cambridge after the war, supporting himself, apart from an ex-serviceman's pension, by taking part-time jobs. His distance from the class above is abundantly clear: 'When finally I did arrive in Cambridge, I still didn't see myself there, never felt at home. Statutes about not playing marbles on the Senate House steps, that kind of thing, never made me giggle cosily; they merely irritated me.'[60] A.J. Cronin took himself through medical training at Glasgow University on scholarships and part-time earnings. After a number of provincial appointments, he took up a practice in Bayswater in West London. By sheer chance he managed to save the life of a rich old lady, mother of a buyer for a West End fashion house (who to Cronin, at least, projected a very upper-class image). As Cronin narrates, 'calls began to come in, at first gradually, then with increasing frequency, from parts of London outside my own district, and far superior to it in social standing.'[61] 'For one who had hitherto been struggling in a middle-class surgery for driblets of five shillings and even half-a-crown this turn of events was a godsend.' 'More and more I was preoccupied by my "high-class" patients, less and less by the ordinary working people who came to the side door.'[62] These are the images of a very middle-class figure, but one who may be moving up. In fact, Cronin was now aiming for Harley Street; had he made it he might well have been absorbed into the upper class. As it was, an ulcer forced him to give up medicine, and he turned instead to writing. Though he became successful and very rich, he seems to have preferred to keep clear of upper-class society.[63]

Certainly, no one has described Cronin as Nevinson and Garnett described Galsworthy. It is to Galsworthy's literary representations that I now turn. In the Edwardian period Galsworthy wrote a group of novels, *The Man of Property*, *The Country House*, *Fraternity* and *The Patrician*, which in a letter he referred to as his 'four *class* novels' (Galsworthy's own emphasis).[64] Now the famous opening sentence of *The Man of Property* makes clear what class is being dealt with: 'Those privileged to be present at a family festival of the Forsytes have seen that charming and instructive sight—an upper-middle-class family in full plumage.'[65] *The Patrician* explicitly concerns a class above. Yet Galsworthy made it clear to Garnett that he was already aware that the upper class contained more than just the aristocracy: 'I am not so tolerant at heart of the aristocrat as you—because their seeming class qualities of simplicity, consideration, high spirit, and a sort of stoicism, are partly the outcome of life's kindness to them, and partly artificially fostered for their own self-preservation. Scratch them and you soon find the Squire or bourgeois.'[66] Then:

The so-called 'well-bred' man and woman is now a very wide class, and only those who have been through the fashionable public-school and Varsity curriculum as I have (and with an inner eye as mine is) can appreciate the at once levelling and formative power of that system. It has brought aristocracy (who all pass through it now) completely off its perch. I have left out of the enclosed list [sent to Garnett to prove Galsworthy's close acquaintanceship with true aristocrats] *nouveau* or *parvenu* aristocracy (expect perhaps half-a-dozen); they're nearly all old-stock, but I assure you I could parallel them two or three times over with 'well-bred' men and women quite untitled from whom you couldn't tell them. A slight extra regularity of feature; an ounce or two more high spirit; a harder and less receptive turn of mind is common to all this class which has blood in it; but it's by no means confined to titled gents.[67]

During the war Galsworthy decided to take up again the fortunes of the Forsyte family, and following up *The Man of Property* of the previous decade, with *The Indian Summer of a Forsyte*, he then with further novels extended what now became known as *The Forsyte Saga* through to 1920. The 1922 one-volume edition contained a Forsyte family tree which followed quite closely (though far from slavishly) Galsworthy's own: descended from eighteenth-century farming stock, the first Jolyon Forsyte was a builder who married the daughter of a country solicitor; of his sons, old Jolyon became an immensely rich tea merchant, and James set up his own firm of solicitors. This family tree is eminently believable; it would, on the other hand, be impossible to envisage any family tree attached to the dramatic fantasies of Masterman's *England After the War*. The opening of the second-last chapter of the final volume, *To Let*, stresses both the rise of the upper-middle-class Forsytes into the upper class proper, and, more important, the way in which they had already become indistinguishable from the upper class into which Fleur Forsyte is marrying:

The October paragraphs describing the wedding of Fleur Forsyte to Michael Mont hardly conveyed the symbolic significance of this event. In the union of the great-granddaughter of 'Superior Dosset' [the builder, 1770–1850] with the heir of a ninth baronet was the outward and visible sign of that merger of class in class which buttresses the political stability of a realm. The time had come when the Forsytes might resign their natural resentment against a 'flummery' not theirs by birth, and accept it as the still more natural due of their possessive instincts. Besides, they had to mount to make room for all those so much more newly rich. In that quiet but tasteful ceremony in Hanover Square, and afterward among the furniture in Green Street, it had been impossible for those not in the know to distinguish the Forsyte troop from the Mont contingent—so far away was 'Superior Dosset' now. Was there, in the crease of his trousers, the expression of his moustache, his accent, or the shine on his top-hat, a pin to chose [sic] between Soames and the ninth baronet himself? Was not Fleur as self-possessed, quick, glancing, pretty, and hard as the liveliest Musteham, Mont, or Charwell filly present. If anything, the Forsytes had it in dress and looks and manners. They had become 'upper-class' and now their name would be formally recorded in the Stud Book, their money joined to land.[68]

Galsworthy continued the saga of the now upper-class Forstyes in a further series *A Modern Comedy* (collected edition, 1929). In the preface he declared that his concern was with 'that tenth or so of the population whose eyes are above the property line',[69] though presumably he did not really believe that the upper class extended to 10 per cent of the population. Divisions and snobbishnesses within the upper class are recognised. The Monts are descended from lawyers in the reign of James I, yet Michael Mont is a junior partner in a publishing firm. In this production of the older Galsworthy, the political discussions are trivial, and the celebrations of 'Englishness' bogus: but the social observation is acute, and confirms the image of an extended upper class derived from other sources.

Britain in the Inter-War Years: Realities

This section endeavours to show that the sorts of individual who belonged to that upper class whose existence was perceived by people of the time, did indeed have disproportionately easy access to positions of power. From the 1920s onwards membership of the House of Commons is not of itself necessarily of great significance: the individuals to note are those who secure winnable seats at a remarkably early age, who remain in active politics for long continuous periods, who move into the circles from which ministers are chosen, or who, at the very least, form influential backbench groupings.

If we take the Cabinet formed immediately after the last general election of our period, that of 1935, we find that out of a total of twenty, twelve quite definitely belonged to this upper class, two are on their way into it, while only six are clearly not upper-class. There were five undoubted aristocrats: Lord Londonderry, the Privy Seal, a direct descendant of Viscount Castlereagh, the famous statesman of the Napoleonic era, educated at Eton and Sandhurst, and entering the House of Commons at the age of twenty-eight; the Secretary for War, the Viscount Halifax, son of the second Viscount and of the only daughter of the eleventh Earl of Devon, educated at Eton and Christ Church Oxford, and married to the younger daughter of the fourth Earl of Onslow (the *Dictionary of National Biography* tells us that: 'The loyalty which at his wedding burdened him with a solid gold cup nearly two feet high as a tribute from the tenantry helped to ensure his election in January 1910 as Conservative Member of Parliament for Ripon'—he was then twenty-eight); Lord Eustace Percy, Minister without Portfolio, the son of the seventh Duke of Northumberland and of the daughter of the eighth Duke of Argyle, and educated at Eton and Christ Church Oxford; Oliver Stanley, President of the Board of Education, son of the seventeenth Earl of Derby, MP at the age of twenty-eight; and W. Ormsby-Gore, First Commissioner of Works, whose father was the third Baron Harlech and mother a daughter of the tenth Marquis of Huntley. Next came four members of the landed gentry: Sir Samuel Hoare, the Foreign Secretary, from an old Norfolk banking family, educated at Harrow and New College Oxford, first entered Parliament aged twenty-nine; Sir Philip Cunliffe-Lister, immediately elevated to the peerage as Viscount Swinton, Secretary of State for Air, son of a Yorkshire landowner, educated at Winchester and Oxford, called to the Bar, then entered Parliament when just into his thirties; Anthony Eden, Minister responsible for League of Nations affairs, whose memoirs of his youth form an elegant lament for Edwardian aristocratic society;[70] and Sir B. Eyres-Monsell (now created Viscount Monsell), at the Admiralty, son of a Lieutenant-Colonel and grandson on his mother's side of Sir E. Ogle, the sixth baronet. Lastly, three members of the successful nineteenth-century industrial and business class: Stanley Baldwin, the Prime Minister, whose father had headed the family iron foundry, and who was himself educated at prep school, Harrow and Trinity College, Cambridge, eventually (aged forty-one) inheriting his father's safe parliamentary seat;

Neville Chamberlain, son of the famous Birmingham industrialist Joseph Chamberlain by his second wife, educated at Rugby, though not at Oxbridge; and Sir Godfrey Collins, Secretary of State for Scotland, head of the famous Scottish publishing company.

Leading backbenchers of the time were, from the older generation, Winston Churchill, scion of the Marlborough family and the leading dissident of the day, and from the younger generation, Harold Macmillan, the dominant figure in the influential Middle Opinion Movement of the 1930s.[71] A member of the successful Victorian publishing family, Macmillan was educated at Eton, and then at Balliol. Though born in an elegant house in Cadogan Place, or perhaps because of this, he was very aware of the existence of a social stratum above his: 'At the top of our street was a large mansion, Chelsea House. . . . To us humbler neighbours, Chelsea House was a kind of baronial castle only outmatched in importance by Buckingham Palace . . .'.[72] Whatever fractions may have existed within the class to which Macmillan belonged, they scarcely created barriers as he sought in the immediate post-war years to avoid going into the family firm, and instead went to Canada on the staff of the Duke of Devonshire, newly appointed Governor-General: 'My mother . . . was a long-standing friend of Lady Edward Cavendish, the Duke's mother . . .'.[73] The trip led even further, for Macmillan married the Duke's daughter, Dorothy Cavendish. Immediately, he moved into the world of high politics, with a Conservative seat being provided.

The argument, it must be repeated, is not that the upper class I have identified ruled, but that individual members of this class had disproportionate access to positions of power. The argument is neatly borne out by the figures of those entering the higher civil service by open competition (there was very little promotion from below): in 1929 over a quarter came from the Clarendon schools; by 1939 this figure had dropped slightly to about a fifth. In both cohorts the proportion of Clarendon school men in the most senior positions (Secretaries and Deputy Secretaries) was as high as a third.[71] The Permanent Head of the Civil Service throughout the inter-war years was Sir Warren Fisher, whose upper-class education, as well as his handsome good looks, are stressed in the *Dictionary of National Biography*.[75]

Apart from Fisher, the other most powerful *éminence grise* in inter-war Britain, was Montagu Norman, Governor of the Bank of England. The nice mix of banking, commercial, landed and professional interests which he had behind him put him slightly above a Galsworthy or a Forsyte, yet the class characteristics are recognisably of the same order. Montagu's paternal grandfather, George Warde Norman, derived his initial fortune from real estate and timber and married into Martin's Bank, thus gaining 'a place among the City aristocracy',[76] eventually becoming a Director of the Bank of England. Montagu's father qualified as a barrister, became a junior partner in a private banking house, and married the daugher of Sir Mark Collett, a Director, in his own right as it were, of the Bank of England. Montagu Norman went to Eton and King's College, Cambridge.

Upper-class dominance of industry is less easy to show: successful industrialists are as often on their way into the upper class as already members of it.[77] Equally, upper-class figures with a background in the higher professions might well take powerful positions in industry. The self-made first Lord Leverhulme was unsuccessful in his attempt to pass on the chairmanship of the Unilever combine to his son; instead the post was taken by Sir Francis D'arcy Cooper, of the family accountacy firm of Cooper Bros & Co.[78] Dr Charlotte Erickson has told us that, 'one of the most significant trends in the education of steel manufacturers has been an increase in gravitation to the particular schools which are today rcognised as public schools.'[79] The power behind Imperial Chemical Industries, Sir Alfred Mond, became as Lord Melchett a Tory grandee later fêted (see below) by an American aristocrat; his father had been born in Germany, but made enough money as a chemicals manufacturer in this country to send both of his sons to public school and university.[80] ICI boards exemplify perfectly the way in which members of the upper class easily played musical chairs between government and big business. Among those who served in the inter-war years were Rufus Isaacs, first Marquis of Reading, who had been Lord Chief Justice, and then, for five years, Viceroy of India (his son, incidentally, had married Alfred Mond's daughter Eva), Lord Birkenhead (the former F.E. Smith, successively in the 1920s Lord Chancellor and Secretary for India), Lord Weir, the Scottish shipping magnate and pillar of Toryism, and Sir John Anderson, Permanent Under-Secretary at the Home Office, and Director of the Government's Preparations against the General Strike; ICI's first treasurer was recruited from the Inland Revenue.[81] Let me end with the figure with whom I began, Sir Ian Fraser, a Governor of the BBC, and Director of several companies. Fraser's is a classic instance of the imperial connection. His money came from South Africa, where he was reared till the age of eight when he was sent to a prep school and then to Marlborough. He was blinded during the First World War, entered Parliament as a Conservative (at a very early age), asked a question about the BBC and thus became instantly recognised as an expert; he also trained as a barrister and was a director of several companies both in Britain and South Africa.[82]

France in the Inter-War Years: Images

The labels *classes ouvrières* and *classes moyennes* (as also *classes paysannes*) were in widespread use in France in the inter-war years, but there was no acceptable analogue of 'upper class'. One sweeping categorisation simply distinguished between *les classes populaires* and *les classes bourgeoises*.[83] Academic writers concerned with a precise delineation of the social structure adopt slightly different categories and groups of categories, but in fact the sense of an upper class not utterly different from the one we have studied in Britain does emerge; most critically, all commentators are able to separate out a *grande bourgeoisie* from the middle classes, the intermediate classes, or the medium and petty bourgeoisie.[84] Having identified a working class, a peasant class, and a middle class, François Simiand, in his famous lectures on political economy given at the Sorbonne in the late 1920s, identified, fourthly, the *classe bourgeoise*, into which he said the aristocracy had merged. He reckoned this bourgeois class at 5 per cent of the population: however, he felt it could be subdivided into the petty bourgeoisie, who were really *the* middle class (as distinct from the middle classes he had already identified), the medium bourgeoisie, the grand bourgeoisie, and, above these, 'a category of magnates, who have special traits of their own but also share common bourgeois characteristics'. If the boundary lines are not completely clear, the sense of there being at the top a mixed social grouping sharing common characteristics, is.[85]

An interesting collection in the Municipal Archives in Strasbourg offers insights into the self-imagery of Alsation notables in our period. Ferdinand Dollinger was a member of the French Senate, and a leading figure among Alsatian Protestants, the bulk of whom were functionaries and members of the white-collar class generally. A fellow Protestant wrote to Dollinger in November 1932 agreeing that many among them were 'proud of their quarters of nobility', adding that he himself represented 'the third generation of his family'.[86]

What really did it mean to be noble? In his *The Nobility* (1938), Jougla de Morenas included both the 'true nobility', from which he endeavoured to filter out 'unscrupulous adventurers, useless fops and the presumptuously newly enriched', and the 'excellent bourgeoisie', only barred by 'Republican principles from the legitimate pursuit of ennoblement'.[87] A similar view of a class embracing both those with actual titles and those who, were titles still on offer in republican France, would have earned them, is presented by M. le duc de Lévis Mirepoix, President of *L'Association d'Entraide de la noblesse Française* (founded in 1932): in every civilised country, said Lévis Mirepoix, 'individuals sought to give their scattered achievements a permanent form' and thus the nobility 'was never a closed caste: it was a continuous creation'.[88] The images presented here suggest a small, but not tiny, upper-bourgeois class which embraces the titled nobility.

At the other extreme was the notion of France having a tiny ruling class of '200 families'. *Crapouillot*, the witty and urbane French equivalent of such British journals as *Illustrated* and *Picture Post*, devoted an entire special issue in March 1936 to 'the 200 families'. What sort of people were thought to head these 200 families was made clear in the article '200 and Something Families':

Impeccable automobiles flash each day through the streets of Paris carrying groups of sedate gentlemen . . .

You have just been looking in on the members of the Holy Alliance, the unknown masters. They are called Dupont-Durand, or Baron-Durand, the name does not evoke in you anything completely precise. All the same, if an unknown prompt whispered to you: the big one with the bowler hat and the tooth-brush moustache is the President of your Electricity company, his companion controls the Banks X and Y, the one who is squeezed up on the flap seat represents the Z Insurance Group, certain precise images would then jump into your mind, good God, Yes!—the payment of your gas bill, the collection of your theft insurance. And your whisperer would have been able to complete your education by pointing out that the electricity gentleman is also the chemicals and oils gentleman, that he of the life insurances also holds railways, armaments and dress design, and astonishing and contradictory mixture. . . .

They are intelligent, no doubt about that. Their youth was studious, they passed out from the *grandes écoles*. Some are your elected representatives, but yes, others come from ambassadorships, the army, the ministries: admire their ribbons of honour.[89]

Actually, if you follow the logic of the *Crapouillot* article you arrive at quite a large upper class, including the old Paris upper bourgeoisie of *fonctionnaires* and *intellectuels*, and the industrial barons.[90]

Such an upper class of select, but mixed origins is clearly represented in French literature of the time. The first volume of Maurice Druon's trilogy *The End of Mankind*, written just after the end of the Second World War, but set in the inter-war years, is entitled *The Great Families* and is, incidentally, dedicated to La Marquise Brissac, Princesse d'Arenberg. On the opening pages we are introduced to the Marquis de La Monnerie, to Jean de La Monnerie, 'the celebrated poet and academician', to the Baron Noel Schoudler, Regent of the Bank of France, and to his father Siegfried Schoudler, founder of the Bank Schoudler. Throughout the trilogy we are in the world of high finance and high politics: a main character is the government minister, Simon Lachaume. The opening of the third volume, *Rendezvous in Hell* describes Paris in the late spring, the 'Season': the police are mobilised to facilitate the grand receptions 'of an academician, a newspaper director, a duchess, a senior barrister (*batonnier*), a big banker. . . .'[91] The English connection, apparently so essential to the image of French high life, features in the form of the rather ineptly named Lord Peemrose. The trilogy ends with the war and in the 'epilogue' Simon Lachaume recognises that it will destroy a society he himself has no wish to survive: he had been *'le parlementaire mondier*, who attended private views, masked balls, and first nights'.[92]

The sense of a separate and distinctive upper class is also clearly evident in the twenty-seven volumes of Jules Romains' *Les Hommes de bonne volonté* (1932–36). In the novel which re-starts the story line at the end of the First World War we encounter immediately the rich industrialist Haverkamp in discussion with Turpin, a prosperous architect who wears English cheviot suits, and Serge Vazar an interior decorator. Haverkamp is discussing his plans for his Paris town mansion and château in the country.[93] Vazar has two or three commissions for the old aristocracy, but since, 'though fussy, they are never in a hurry', he can also fit in Haverkamp's requirements. Thus again the image is of an upper bourgeois upper class, with a small, and perhaps not very effective, aristocratic element within it. As with *The End of Mankind* we are constantly traversing a world of industry, finance, politics, grand-scale shop-keeping (Nodiard of the *Palais du Linge* could be modelled on the real-life owner of *Printemps*, Pierre Laguionie).[94] Nodiard's son both goes to Communist Party meetings in working-class Paris and belongs to an exclusive dining club in London.[95]

A mannered, aristocratic world is presented in Jean Renoir's celebrated film, *La Règale du jeu* (1938). But the aristocratic figure who presides over the house-party is in fact a *nouveau riche*, and among the guests are an heroic aviator who has just flown the Atlantic, and the avuncular intellectual, Octave, played by Renoir himself, who fits readily into the aristocratic fun-and-games. Behind the upper-class life-style lies the extended upper class.

France in the Inter-War Years: Reality

Let us first glance at Raymond Poincaré, Prime Minister then President of the Republic before the war; elder statesman and several times Prime Minister after it. He was, the *French Biographical Dictionary* tells us, born 'in the heart of a family from the excellent Lorraine bourgeoisie, rich in men of high value'. His father was a former pupil of the École Polytechnic and an engineer at the Ponts et Chaussées, then Inspector General of the Hydrolique. Poincaré himself, first of all, went to the *lycée* at Bar-le-Duc where he was born, but then, important point, he went to the famous Louis le Grand *lycée* in Paris, became a barrister at the age of twenty-six, was made a *chef-de-cabinet*, and at the age of twenty-seven was elected to Parliament. Throughout he was very close to the great iron and steel barons, the de Wendel family, though himself from an administrative not an industrial capitalist family.[96]

The dominance of positions of political power by members of the upper class (nobility and grand bourgeoisie together) is very apparent in a table prepared by Professor Dogan:[97]

| | Social origin of Deputies (%) | | Social origin of Ministers (%) |
	1919	1936	1899–1940
Nobility	10	5	4
High bourgeoisie	30	24	37
Middle bourgeoisie	35	36	33
Small bourgeoisie	15	20	17
Working class	10	15	7
No information	—	—	2

Membership of the French Chamber of Deputies did not necessarily entail great political power, and indeed it was probably more of a middle-class body than Professor Dogan's figures suggest, since many of his high bourgeoisie were probably perceived by themselves and by French society as being middle-class rather than upper-class.

But if we look at the twelve individuals who served as Prime Minister during the 1930s (some of them several times) we find that exactly half of these belong quite unambiguously to the upper class as I have described it. This would be to exclude both Léon Blum, who might almost be reckoned part of the intellectual fraction of the upper class, and Edouard Herriot, who was a *notable* in the provincial middle class.[98] Camille Chautemps came from an old established Savoy family. His uncle was a Senator, and his father both a former minister and vice-president of the Senate. He was educated at the lycée Charlemagne and then at the lycée Marceau at Chârtres, where his mother was a substantial property owner. André Tardieu, was even more distinctively upper-class: 'spoiled child, privileged child', as one of his biographers put it, 'André Tardieu was the *gosse de riche* who went to play in the Parc Monceau'.[99] In 1896 Tardieu's father had published a copious volume tracing the family's history as leaders of Parisian society back to the seventeenth century; his mother was Charlotte d'Arpentigny de Malleville. The father of Joseph Paul-Boncour was doctor to Élie-Roger-Louis de Talleyrand-Périgord, Prince de Chalais, duc de Périgord, and belonged himself to a family of doctors, notaries and administrators. Paul-Boncour's mother belonged to a monarchist and Catholic family which traced its lineage back to William the Conqueror (British aristocrats are not alone in doing this).[100] Albert Sarraut belonged to an important family from the south-west, closely associated with the powerful political journal, *La Dépêche de Toulouse*; he himself became a Deputy in 1902 at the age of thirty, and his brother Maurice became a Senator in 1913. The family of Pierre-Etienne Flandin (formerly called Flandin des Aubues) rated three other entries in the *French Biographical Dictionary*. His grandfather's grandfather had been a doctor; his father was first a Deputy and then a Senator. He himself studied at the lycée Carnot, took a diploma from the École des Sciences Politiques, a doctorate in law, and became an advocate at the Court of Appeal in Paris. He was elected Deputy at the age of twenty-five. Finally, Paul Reynaud, Prime Minister just after the outbreak of war, came from a long-established family of prosperous peasants in the French Alps. His grandfather was mayor of the village of St Paul and his great uncle a doctor. His father made a fortune in Mexico, returned to take a flat in Paris, build himself a country mansion, and married the daughter of the most important man in the valley, a banker and mayor of

Barcelonnette; this marriage Reynaud described as 'a social promotion'.[101] While the father continued with his Mexican enterprises, the young Reynaud was brought up in Paris where he went to the same school as the Rothschilds. At his father's insistence he did two years at the École des Hautes Études Commercials, then, as was fitting in a high bourgeois member of the upper class, he turned to the law. He also travelled a great deal in England, and was much given to dropping little hints about his familiarity with British ways.[102]

Even after changes carried through by the Popular Front government, the Bank of France remained a private institution dominated by the major shareholders and still very much under the influence of the traditional families who had sat in 'the armchairs of the regents', the Vernes, the Mallets, the Rothschilds, the Wendels.[103] Similar figures dominated the vast nationalised enterprises. Although the *Crapouillot* article already referred to indulged in rhetorical exaggeration, it was a fine piece of investigative journalism, which built up a convincing biographical description of the families overlapping in their control of state enterprises, financial institutions, private industries and international corporations.[104] The massive study by Jean-Noël Jeanneney (himself, it may be noted, the scion of an established upper-class family of public servants and academics) of *François de Wendel and the Republic: Money and Power 1914–1940* establishes both the extent of, and the limits on, the power of members of the French grand bourgeoisie.[105]

America in the Inter-War Years: Images

Compared with the French, American academic writing on class in the inter-war years is very inconclusive. We are given either an economic interpretation, representing American society as being divided between 'capital' and 'labor', with the 'middle classes' in between, or an anthropological approach, based on the detailed study of small towns in which, of course, the upper class would not be seen dead.[106] Informal images are more helpful. Most of the major American conurbations had their *Social Registers*, which being private, market-oriented productions, can be seen as reliable guides as to which families genuinely were thought to belong to an upper class: at the end of the inter-war period a total of 38,450 families were in the various social registers,[107] something around 1 per cent of the population as a whole.

We find Roosevelt's black valet writing of the American Ambassador to Brazil as 'indeed nice from an aristocratic old Virginia family'.[108] Roosevelt and Dean Atcheson, son of the Episcopal Bishop of Connecticut, had an immediate bond in that they had both been to Groton, though there is not the lingering in Atcheson's reminiscences on the old school tie that there would have been in comparable British autobiography.[109] Indeed, the 1932 Presidential election campaign provides a classic instance of the way in which polemical literature, wittingly conveying diametrically opposite messages, in fact unwittingly conveys the same class image. The 'Friends of Franklin D. Roosevelt' praise their candidate for his colonial ancestry and traditions of public service; Republican supporters describe Roosevelt as having been born with a gold spoon in his mouth and having been dressed as a child in little Lord Fauntleroy suits—Roosevelt, they argue, has lived a life separate from ordinary people.[110] Harold L. Ickes, Roosevelt's Secretary of State for the Interior, showed upper-class pride, and, above all, upper-class admiration for most things British. Describing a British Embassy party in September 1940, he wrote:

I was the ranking guest and sat on Lord Lothian's right. On my right sat Lord Melchett. Lord Stonehaven was another guest who had recently arrived from England. . . .
    I was tremendously impressed with the self-control of these Britishers. . . .
    I was greatly impressed with Lord Melchett personally. . . . He is a widely-read and cultured English Gentleman—the kind we don't often produce over here where we have a much more narrow range of historical and current events and where the chief consideration is the making of money. . . .[111]

But those who made money had at their disposal well-trodden paths to the upper class if they cared to take them. Patrick Kennedy, saloon-keeper son of an Irish immigrant, was definitely no proper Bostonian. At the beginning of the century he sent his son Joseph across town to an upper-class Protestant day school, the Boston Latin School. When Joseph Kennedy himself addressed the school's tercentenary dinner in 1935, he made the sort of noises which would not have been out of place in a similar English context:

> To strangers I could not possibly convey the reasons for the powerful and sweet hold which the School has upon my affections. It would be like trying to explain to strangers why I love my family. . . . the Latin school as we know it was a shrine that somehow seemed to make us all feel that if we could stick it out at the Latin school, we were made of just a little better stuff than the rest of the follows of our own age who were attending what we always thought were easier schools . . .[112]

By this time Joseph Kennedy had progressed through Harvard, where he roomed in the exclusive Harvard Yard. With the right connections, and elements of the right manner, Kennedy proceeded to make a great deal of money very fast. Acceptable within Roosevelt's upper-class circles, he was appointed Chairman of the Securities and Exchange Commission, the body charged with the job of monitoring business deals. The upward movement was legitimated with his designation as American Ambassador to London—or almost legitimated. At the outbreak of War Kennedy was still awaiting the full acceptance which would come when the family ceased to be referred to as Irish-American, but simply as American.[113]

There are some sharp images of an upper class, distinctive, and 'less extended' than that of Britain or France in Hollywood films; indeed I would cite Hollywood in support of the contention that Americans are not as unaware of class as is so often said (most recently by Pessen)—though it is true their awareness, in keeping with actual social realities, is lower than that of their European counterparts. Very often the major class line presented is that between an upper class and a middle class of journalists, professors, doctors; sometimes we see the highly successful lawyer beginning to make it into the upper class. In *The Mad Miss Manton*, Barbara Stanwyck is the upper-class lady, Henry Fonda the ordinary reporter. He is roughed-up by a group of society ladies: in referring to this event he remarks that he had 'just been inducted into the Junior League'. The eponymous *Counsellor at Law* remarks that he is supposed to be a famous lawyer, and that if he takes their brief 'people from old families think I'm doing them a favour'. It becomes clear that one of the old families he had in mind is that of the President of the United Steel Corporation.

The Seatons in *Holiday* (1938) are described as one of America's top sixty families. Cary Crant plays John Case the son of a grocer from Baltimore, who has worked his way through Harvard and who has also worked in a laundry, a steel mill and on a garbage truck. His closest friends are an old couple, who indicate lowly status by taking off galoshes and shoes when they come to a formal party at the Seaton household. The husband is in fact a university professor, but 'teaching at university doesn't pay me very much'. Case has become engaged to Julia Seaton, but finds her upper-class manner increasingly hard to take, despite the fact that her father suggests a honeymoon in London, together with a job in a British bank or a French firm, to be followed in due course by a house full of servants on 64th Street. Case leaves for Europe with the professor and his wife, but is joined by the rebellious younger Seaton daughter, played by Katherine Hepburn. Cary Grant has not joined the upper class whose barriers have remained intact; it is Katherine Hepburn who has come down the social scale to join him.

The point was made even more strongly in *Philadelphia Story* (1940). The aristocratic Philadelphia lady, played by Katherine Hepburn, has been divorced from another aristocrat, Cary Grant, and it is into this situation that James Stewart, as a journalist, blunders. When James Stewart remarks that the library contains a book written by him, Katherine Hepburn remarks that her grandfather had built the library. She is now engaged to a former coalminer turned businessman—an admirable character and the epitome of the American success story, you might think, save that in the film he is portrayed as a narrow-minded bounder. 'You've got all the arrogance of your class,' he bursts out at one point against Cary Grant. Much of the plot centres on the night out which Katherine Hepburn and James Stewart have together. But, in the end, when the lower-class suitor is brushed aside, his place is taken, not by James Stewart, but, in a perfect re-matching of class backgrounds, by Cary Grant. James Stewart sticks strictly within his class and marries his faithful colleague and companion.

Platinum Blonde (1931) features the upper-class Schuyler

48

family. A crack journalist, played by Robert Williams, is sent to investigate a salacious story linking the Schuyler family with a chorus girl. Setting out confidently, the journalist who has the pleasantly common name of Stuart Smith, declares that he knows these 'blue noses'. His first encounters are with the Schuyler lawyer, who demonstrates his upper-class status by speaking with an anglified accent, and the Schuyler butler who, a most important point, demonstrates the status of the Schuyler family by being a genuine Englishman. The lawyer intimidates Smith by reminding him that he is a stockholder in the newspaper, and that further he knows Smith's managing editor: 'Yale '21 I believe', he says. But Ann Schuyler, the platinum blonde of the title, played by Jean Harlow, decides she wants to marry Smith; she also seeks to turn him into a real upper-class gentleman. Smith's Yale '21 editor summarises the class relationship: 'Ann Schuyler's in the blue book, you're not even in the phone book.' After the marriage, apparently unconsummated as so often in American films of these days, Smith realises his mistake in trying to cross the boundaries of class, while the platinum blonde decides that it would after all be better to be married to her upper-class lawyer. Now sticking sensibly with his own social class, Smith marries a fellow journalist.

In *Sullivan's Travels* (1941) Joel McCrea plays John L. Sullivan, a Hollywood film director who, in common with his two financial associates, shares those attributes which I have already suggested may legitimately be termed upper-class. Sullivan was educated in a private boarding school, and is described by one of his associates as class I: the same associate also concludes a piece of dialogue with: 'You're a gentleman to admit it—but then you are anyway.' Sullivan—clinching symbol once again—has an English butler *and* an English valet.

American novels offer some useful hints as well, and there are very clear images of the upper-class east coast world of the well-educated young lady in the novels in the trilogy by John Dos Passos, *USA*. In *Nineteen Nineteen* we encounter the daughter of a prominent Dallas attorney:

Next fall Dad took her north for a year in a finishing school in Lancaster, Pennsylvania. She was excited on the trip up on the train and loved every minute of it, but Miss Tynge's was horrid and the girls were all northern girls and so mean and made fun of her clothes and talked about nothing but Newport and Southampton, and matinée idols she'd never seen; she hated it.[114]

In *The Big Money*, Mary French is the daughter of a Colorado doctor, her best friend being the daughter of a much more prosperous and powerful Jewish-Chicago lawyer:

At Vassar the girls she knew were better dressed than she was and had uppety finishing school manners, but for the first time in her life she was popular. . . .
   It was all spoiled the second year when Ada came to Vassar. . . . Ada had gotten so loud and Jewish and noisy, and her clothes were too expensive and never just right.[115]

Malcolm Cowley has suggested that much of Scott Fitzgerald's work is concerned 'with the relationship between social classes', and he identifies the two social classes concerned as 'the middle class' and the 'very rich' adding 'sometimes the family is Southern, in which case it needn't be so rich, since a high social status can exist in the South without great wealth'. Tom Buchanan and his wife Daisy come into the upper-class category in *The Great Gatsby*; Nick, the narrator, and Gatsby himself do not.[116]

America in the Inter-War Years: Reality

While Suzanne Keller's main objective was to demonstrate the existence of 'strategic élites' she had, earlier, demonstrated the dominant influence of colonial families on major business positions: for the inter-war period something like 60–70 per cent of American business leaders were drawn from this core group of the upper class.[117] Business recruitment is less amenable to the forces of pluralism, sectionalism and democracy than political advancement. Only one President in this period, Roosevelt, was indisputably a member of the upper class, though Woodrow Wilson was certainly on the lower fringes of it: of Roosevelt, Edward Pessen has written: 'FDR had as little difficulty as his cousin [Theodore Roosevelt, in the pre-war era] in entering politics and quickly winning a success that appears to have been due above all to his family's fame and standing.'[118] Upper-class power and cohesion shows itself from time to time, and never more obviously than in Roosevelt's first administration, many of whose members were Republicans. John G. Winant, one of the most important organisers of the social security programme, came from an aristocratic New York family, was educated at Princeton, and joined himself to an aristocratic Princeton family by marrying the daughter of Eleanor Roosevelt's father's law partner. Francis Biddle was another Republican grandee who joined the Roosevelt team. Among other close advisors were A.A. Berle, Jnr a corporation lawyer featured in the pages of the *New York Social Register*, Raymond Morley, a criminologist and Professor of Public Law at Columbia, and Gerrard Swope, Head of General Motors. His first Secretary of the Treasury (later succeeded by Dean Atcheson) was William H. Woodin, a Republican magnate from the American Car and Foundry Motor Company, a Director of eight other institutions including the Federal Reserve Bank of New York, and a listee in the *Social Register*. Secretary for Labor was that perfect Bostonian 'clubwoman', Frances Perkins. Secretary of State, Cordell Hull, was not part of the national upper class, though an important figure in Tennessee where he was a barrister, judge, congressman and senator.[119]

Since the 1950s

By the 1970s, many academic works were openly recognising the existence of an American upper class.[120] The major general study, *Social Standing in America: New Dimensions of Class*, by Richard P. Coleman and Lee Rainwater, postulated a very extended upper class (probably too extended in that it included those others would term 'upper-middle'): 'in the world of the Upper Americans there are three thematic subdivisions: the old rich of aristocratic family name, the new rich—this genera-tion's success élite—and the college-educated professional and managerial class of more moderate success'.[121] In the informal sources there is a growing sense of the existence of a unified national upper class. In her Horace Mann lecture for 1960 on the 'Psychology of the Child in the Middle Class', Alison Davis recognised a social hierarchy which distinguished 'the upper class' from 'the middle class'. Her paper was about the hardships of the middle-class child:

unlike individuals in the 'leisure class' or aristocracy, who inherit their positions of distinction in both the social and financial worlds, the middle-class individual usually has to achieve his position in the manufacturing or business world, and always must achieve it in the professional world. He must strive toward the attainment of long-postponed goals, and compete effectively with others who are similarly striving.[122]

The self-image of the upper class can, in a manner surprising to Europeans, be seen in the page upon page devoted to society weddings, in the *New York Times*. Early in 1960 *Life* interviewed two young men on 'the Debutante Circuit', David Treherne-Thomas, an off-shoot of the British steel family, Richard Thomas, and Peter Monroe-Smith, great grandson of one of the founders of the L.G. Smith and Brothers Typewriter Company, the latter declaring: 'You must be conservative and carefully groomed. This is what draws the line between real society and the new-rich and we will keep them out at all costs.' In 1975 all the local *Social Registers* were amalgamated into one national *Social Register*. In reporting the celebrated Tarnower murder trial of 1981, the *New York Times* was meticulous in identifying which participants were clearly members of the upper class.[123]

In discussing the earlier period in America I made great use of film. Fashions in the arts, of course, change, and it is curious that while the upper class was being openly written about by sociologists, American films of the post-war period tended to be located elsewhere in society; though with *Class* and *Trading Places* film-makers have at last caught up. In *Here Comes the Groom* (1951), Wilbur Stanley, heir to an old Boston family whose insurance company own 'about half the buildings in Boston', is to marry Emmie, who works in one of the insurance offices, and is daughter of a Boston-Irish fisherman. While the Stanley family view is that the 'Stanleys can't just get married like other people', Emmie claims that she is 'going to learn how to be a lady'. Meantime, the successful (but not, of course, upper-class) Boston reporter, Pete (played by Bing Crosby) gets involved with Stanley's aristocratic cousin. Eventually the wedding ceremony comes along, 'with a guest list like the *Blue Book* and *Who's Who* rolled into one': in the course of the traditional Hollywood marriage cliffhanger, Wilbur drops out and pushes Pete into his place. So middle class sticks with middle class and, more relevant to the present concern, the two aristocrats are free to marry each other. *Giant* presented a more rounded social universe, with a long historical overview running from the 1930s to the 1950s. At the beginning, John Benedict (Rock Hudson) comes from Texas into a Maryland upper-class household—fine mansion, full-dress fox hunt, English country-house breakfast—to buy a horse, and marries the daughter of the family, Lesley (Elizabeth Taylor). The social clash between Benedict, a powerful man in Texas, and Lesley and her traditional upper-class background is beautifully realised. Her accommodation to him, as he engages in further power struggles in Texas, suggests the emergence of a consolidated national upper class. Evidence of the rituals and status of the upper-class life, as also, of course, of the ever-present significance of new wealth is apparent in both *Tony Rome* (1961) and *A New Leaf* (1971). In the first, a former bricklayer, now boss of a major construction company, says that he had had to buy 'class', in the shape of his aristocratic wife. In the latter, the impoverished playboy Walter Mathau must find a rich wife for, as his English butler tells him, 'there is no such thing as genteel poverty here, sir'.

Better to turn to low-brow, formulae novels, which being concerned with success, but not explicitly with class, offer much unwitting testimony on the latter. The best-selling novelist Helen Van Slyke died before completing her tenth novel, *Public Smiles, Private Tears*; however, so secure was the formula, that the publishers had no difficulty in finding a hack to complete the book without the slightest perceptible change in style or story line. A southern upper-class figure appears early in the novel:

Frank Burroughs was twenty-eight when they met, a good-looking young Army lieutenant from Virginia currently stationed on Governors Island, the base just outside New York. Impeccable in his custom-tailored uniforms, Frank was a romantic dream. A well-born family had equipped him with a lightly accented prep-school voice, beautiful manners.

As we learn on the next page: 'he planned to return to Virginia after the war and go into his father's law firm'; he also spoke 'of the kind of gentlemanly life that he looked forward to resuming'.[124] In *Scruples*, by Judith Krantz, subsequently a television series, we meet Billy Ikehorn Orsini in Beverly Hills, but immediately learn of her east coast origins: 'She was thirty-five, sole mistress of a fortune estimated at between two hundred and two hundred and fifty million dollars by the list-makers of the *Wall Street Journal*.' She is about to enter the extravagant boutique which she owns. 'But today she was in too much of a rush to scrutinise any of the details of what her Boston background, for she had been born Wilhelmina Hunnenwell Winthrop of the undiluted Massachussets Bay Colony Strain, caused her to refer to as a "business" rather than as a fantasy she had brought to life by pouring out close to eleven million dollars.'[125] Out of the ten main day-time soap operas running on American television at the end of 1984, two were identified by an American newspaper as being concerned with 'aristocratic' families.[126]

In the French academic literature, the work of Pierre Laroque deserves particular attention, for he was a top functionary who had played a central part in drafting the social policies of both the Vichy régime and the first post-war government. Laroque recognised the emergence in modern society of multiple hierarchies—political, economic, administrative, spiritual and cultural—but argued that these could exist side by side with more traditional, historically determined, hierarchies. Contemporary societies were still made up of social classes which he defined as 'relatively closed groups of unequal rank'.[127] In his four-class model of French society Laroque put at the top the 'governing bourgeoisie', which he took to include upper civil servants, senior managers and the more prestigious liberal professions. Laroque clearly had in mind a quite large and relatively open, governing bourgeoisie. He saw it as embracing elements from the summits of different hierarchies—political, economic, administrative, spiritual and intellectual—as well as from families benefiting from traditional prestige. In contrast to Britain, as he saw it (not quite accurately), the leaders of the various hierarchies did not necessarily come from the same social background.[128] Many studies concentrated solely on this 'governing bourgeoisie'.[129]

Of less formal images, the most clear-cut are those offered in François de Negroni's *La France Noble* (1974). Negroni offered some precise figures though, as so often, the precision loses its gloss the closer one looks. He computed the actual nobility at 50,000 *families*, but added a further 400,000 *individual members* of 'high society', 'imperturbably practising the ancient and modern rites attached to their distinctive condition'.[130] Presumably, if we have 50,000 noble families, we have to multiply that figure by something like four to get the total membership of this group; whether one applies the same multiple to the second figure is less clear. Thus, we could be envisaging here an upper class as high as 3 per cent of the population (which seems right to me), or, of course, it could be as low as 1 per cent if the second figure is meant to include all members of families belonging to 'high society'. Negroni gives a marvellous description of those 'ancient and modern rites' which are an essential characteristic of an upper class as described in this essay.[131] In full adulthood, the men will serve in the diplomatic corps, in the top civil service departments, on the boards of major industries, as municipal councillors, or above all, as mayors. They will join the *Jockey Club*, the *Tir Pigeons*, the *Nouveau Cercle*.[132]

For this social class, Jean Baumier is a marvellous unwitting witness, since his explicit intention is to show contemporary France as a democratic meritocracy. In 1924 Raymond Poincaré (to take him up again) had created the Compagnie Française de Pétrole, in the charge of Ernest Mercier. The dominant figure in the post-war years was one of Mercier's nephews, Victor de Metz, described by Baumier as belonging to 'the bonne noblesse', or, in a revealing alternative phrasing, to 'the milieu from which are recruited diplomats, top civil servants, and generals'.[133] Of the Leven family, creators of the massive Perrier combine, Baumier writes: 'in origins, they belong to that bourgeoisie which inhabits elegant town quarters and possesses property in the country.'[134] Ambroise Roux, Director of the nationalised electricity combine, 'is the perfect image of the *grand bourgeois*. He lives in a flat . . . in an elegant quarter of the sixteenth arrondissement: . . . he has for neighbours the la Roche Foucauld and des Noailles'.[135]

Film imagery very much supports the picture emerging from the other sources. The publicity handout for Louis Malle's *Les Amants* (1958) describes Jeanne Moreau as an ordinary provincial housewife.[136] In fact we first see her at a polo match; she lives in a large mansion set in extensive grounds; her husband owns a newspaper; the young archaeologist who gives her a lift in his scruffy little deux chevaux turns out to have cousins well-known in the polo-playing set; there is, in addition, an *English* butler—'Good evening, Cowdry', Jeanne Moreau says to him in English. No ordinary slice of French life this, but a clear representation of that *grande bourgeoisie* whose real-life families are listed in the *Bottin Mondain*. The line between this class and the professional middle class below is clearly delineated in Jacques Becker's *Edouard et Caroline* (1952). Edouard, a concert pianist, lives in a cramped flat with Caroline; she, however, is related to M. Beauchamp who, complete with (slightly camped-up) upper-class Parisian accent inhabits a palatial apartment. The schoolteacher in *Préparez vos Mouchoirs* (1977) has to cope with an upper-class kid deliberately sent to his school to learn popular ways; eventually the boy seduces his wife and the film ends with the schoolteacher and his driving instructor friend vainly pressing their noses against the railings of the upper-class mansion in which the wife is now installed.

Although, recently, there has been much important academic work on the British upper class, the old avoidance of the label has persisted with, for example, such very different commentators as Dudley Seers and Ivan Reid taking the middle class to include everyone not in the working class, or other commentators making decorous use of the label 'upper-middle class'.[137] However, Anthony Crosland, in *The Future of Socialism* (1956), recognised that 'the hierarchies of education, occupational prestige, and style of life' concided in such a way as to create a distinctive upper class.[138] In 1978 the Benwell Community Project in Newcastle upon Tyne published *The Making of a Ruling Class*. The careful, detailed research on which this publication was based brought our very clearly how the descendants of Newcastle's old coal-owning, industrial and banking families of the eighteenth and nineteenth centuries were now powerful components of a nationwide upper class.

Members of these families sat on local authorities, local planning bodies, boards of finance corporations and multinational companies (where they were also substantial shareholders), had been educated at Eton, Harrow, Winchester or Rugby, held substantial family seats in rural Northumberland, belonged to the Northern Counties Club in Newcastle's Hood Street, and (in the case of eighteen families) to such exclusive London clubs as Brooks's, the Turf, Pratt's and the Carlton.[139] Equally fascinating is John Fidler's study of *The British Business Élite: Its Attitudes to Class, Status and Power* (1981). Most of the sample of 130 recognised the existence of an upper class which they saw as consisting of a tiny group of aristocrats, the very wealthy or socialites.[140] Yet, one family businessman perhaps put his finger most firmly on the heart of the issue: 'I am not worried . . . there is nowhere above me that I see that I want to get to, yes. I can't see another [class] above me.'[141]

A key source of upper-class self-imagery is *The British Aristocracy* (1979), by Mark Bence-Jones and Hugh Montgomery-Massingherd which turns out to be a discussion, through a somewhat anachronistic use of the concept of the 'gentlemen', of an extended upper class. Even when Victorian society 'was at its most rigid, a duke and an Indian army subaltern, both being gentlemen, were equal in class, however different they may have been in rank or wealth'.[142] In words which echo those of Nevinson, the authors provide an excellent description of the upper class and the distinctions of status within it:

The British aristocracy has long extended beyond hereditary titles, land and money to include service and professional families that would now be erroneously labelled middle-class. . . .

The law, medicine and other professions, while not conferring aristocratic status quite so definitely as the profession of arms, have been associated with gentlemen ever since the Middle Ages; and by the end of the nineteenth century, the different professions and occupational groups had been fused into a single class by the public schools. . . .

On the whole, of course, the fusion between landed and professional families brought about by the public schools and Services did not go as far as the great territorial magnates, who always tended to form a group apart on account of their wealth. Yet schools like Eton and Harrow did to a certain extent bridge the gap between the greater and lesser aristocracies.[143]

The reference, let me stress, is to the 1970s not to a closed-off historical past: the authors cite contemporary individuals from all walks of life whom they see as belonging to the 'aristocracy' or, more properly, upper class.

This upper class can be seen in certain British films. *Nothing but the Best* (1966) was a satire, yet very shrewd in its stress upon the interrelationship between the forms of upper-class behaviour and the substance of upper-class power. Alan Bates plays a white-collar employee in a large finance company whose chairman (played by Harry Andrews) comes from a very upper-class family. Bates persuades the black sheep of this family (Denholm Elliott) to coach him in upper-class manners and mannerisms. The best degree, he is advised, for him to pretend to have is a history degree: then he simply need say 'bloody' all the time—'bloody Cromwell', 'bloody Napoleon'—and refer to famous historians by their first names—'*Alan* Taylor', '*Hugh* Trevor Roper'. Bates soon learns to exude upper-class arrogance and achieves easy professional success, while, among other things, marrying the chairman's daughter (carefully packing his lower-middle-class parents off out of sight abroad). The suggestion, which was also central to an earlier satire, *I'm All Right Jack* (1959), that a distinctive upper class has continued to exist in Britain and that, while it continues to monopolise positions of economic and political power, it is distinguished more by accent and style (the manners of the gentleman) than political or managerial ability, has a great deal to commend it. *Accident* (1967) was no satire. William (Michael York) is openly recognised as 'an aristocrat', but Dirk Bogarde, the Oxford don, is clearly part of the upper-class world too. The point is made brilliantly when we cut from the exclusive ball game in William's ancestral hall to an Oxford cricket match, less exclusive, but still essentially upper-class. *Room at the Top* (1959) had shown the extended, and extending, upper class. 'Old millionaire Brown' (Donald Wolfitt), the self-made industrialist, has married into the landed gentry (Ambrosine Phillpotts) and the position of daughter Susan (Heather Sears) seems secure. Until predatory Joe Lampton (Laurence Harvey) appears she is destined for Jack Wales (John Westbrook), Cambridge educated, already fully socialised product of earlier industrial wealth. In an early sequence in Joe's new digs the distinction between successful middle-class life and true life at the top is clearly articulated.

The Significance of the Upper Class

The continuing opportunities for individual members of the British and French upper class to exercise power can be seen from their disproportionate representation in the higher civil service in both countries.[144] Recruitment into the Civil Service is much more open in the United States, but then the American Civil Service has relatively low prestige so that it is scarcely a major target for upper-class aspirations. In Margaret Thatcher's first Cabinet, formed in 1979, all but four members belonged to the upper class.[145] Comparison can be made with the seventeen individuals in Giscard's last Cabinet, of whom two belonged to the noble fraction of the upper class: the Minister for the Environment and the Quality of Life, the Count Michel d'Ornano, combining an older service aristocracy with more recent industrial wealth, is listed as the descendant of three marshals of France, prominent in the sixteenth century, the seventeenth century, and the early nineteenth century respectively, and as an industrialist, the son of Count William d'Ornano, also an industrialist; and Giscard d'Estaing himself, whose family had assumed the noble particule in 1926, but who was descended from nineteenth- and twentieth-century senators. A further eleven quite unambiguously belonged to the *grande bourgeoisie*, and included the Minister for Foreign Affairs, Jean Françoise-Poncet, whose financial and business family was almost within the nobility anyway, his father having been a well-known French ambassador; the Minister for Cooperation, Robert Galley, son of a doctor who married the daughter of Marshal Leclerc; and Jacques Barrot, son of a former Deputy and Speaker of the National Assembly, who like so many other members of this Cabinet, entered Parliament at the age of thirty.[146]

Jimmy Carter did not himself come from the upper class, though, L.H. Shoup has persuasively argued, he made great efforts to ingratiate himself with those who did.[147] His

Secretary of State, Cyrus Vance, had had the proper education—Kent School and Yale—and the appropriately lucrative occupations of lawyer and corporation director. Perhaps only two other members of the Cabinet could legitimately be described as having been born into the upper class—Brockman Adams, the Secretary for Transportation, and James Schlesinger, the Secretary for Energy; many others, however, were clearly on their way in.

There is, then, throughout the period studied, a distinctive upper class in all three countries. Within each upper class there are fractions: the Count d'Ornano, was slightly untypical in France; the fictional Billy Ikehorn Orsini was rather exceptional in both descent and wealth. But such people form the essential core of what is a genuine class, and not a mere exclusive élite or cousinage. The term 'upper class', is infinitely preferable to the term 'capitalist class', which does not adequately reflect the complexities of open-market societies, shaped by cultural legacies as well as economic imperatives. Nor is it fully accurate to characterise the upper class by the possession of 'property in production', separating it from a middle class possessed of 'education'.[148] Certain types of education, and certain avocations associated with specialist education, are part-and-parcel of upper-class life.

The French upper class was not destroyed in the collapse of 1940, but it, and French governments, learned a harsh lesson: since the war, French upper-class figures, easily absorbed into government and into industry, have been exceedingly well-educated, and broadly competent to take rational decisions and provide leadership (though one could, of course, object strongly to their position on other grounds). Britain's problem has not been the unique possession of an upper class, but that that upper class has continued to be poorly educated and has shown little understanding of the needs of the contemporary world. The upper class has not had the same dominance in the United States where, to return to Suzanne Keller's formulation, more variables operate in the selection of élites; and where a less extended upper class competing in a pluralistic society against many other interests is less pervasive than a fully extended upper class competing in a more highly-knit society. Today (1985), the ethos which appears to be in the ascendant is that of the lower-middle-class (though excessively rich) President. This President, unlike the British Prime Minister, who comes from a similar social background, has not been swept into any upper-class embrace; perhaps a personal, but more profoundly, a national matter.

Notes

1. The best recent account of the public schools is Jonathan Gathorne-Hardy, *The Public School Phenomenon* (1977).
2. Larry Irvin Bland, 'W. Averell Harriman? Businessman and Diplomat, 1891–1945', University of Wisconsin Ph.D. dissertation, 1972, pp. 9–11.
3. John Westergaard, 'Sociology: The Myth of "Classlessness" ', in R. Blackburn, *Ideology in Social Science*, (1972), pp. 140–1. W. D. Rubinstein, 'Wealth, Elites and the Class Structure of Modern Britain', *Past and Present*, no. 76 (1977), p. 126, refers to Britain as 'an anomalous country'.
4. Suzanne Keller, *Beyond the Ruling Class: Strategic Elites in Modern Society* (1963), p. 205.
5. Gabriel Kolko, *Wealth and Power in America* (1962), pp. 127–8.
6. Kolko, pp. 56–7; Michael Useem, 'The Inner Group of the American Capitalist Class', *Social Problems*, vol. 25 (1978), p. 226.
7. *Who Rules America Now?* (1983), p. 18; cf. Domhoff's *The Power That Be: Processes of Ruling Class Domination in America* (1978), p. 3.
8. *Life*, 28 September, 1959.
9. Laurence H. Shoup, *The Carter Presidency and Beyond: Power and Politics in the 1980s* (1977), p. 17 n. 4.
10. John Scott, *The Upper Classes: Property and Privilege in Britain* (1982), p. 124.
11. Jane Marceau, *Class and Status in France* (1977), p. 129; Pierre Birnbaum *et al.*, *La Classe dirigeante française* (1978), p. 106.
12. Jean Baumier, *Les grandes affaires français: des 200 familles aux 200 managers* (1967), esp. p. 242.
13. Adeline Daumard, 'Wealth and Affluence in France since the Beginning of the Nineteenth Century', in W.D. Rubinstein (ed.), *Wealth and the Wealthy in the Modern World* (1980), p. 120.
14. Rubinstein, *op. cit.*, p. 18.
15. *Ibid.*, p. 54.
16. Edward Pessen, 'Social Structure and Politics in American History', *American Historical Review*, vol. 87, no. 5, December 1982, p. 1296. This article is also a valuable bibliographical guide to works I do not have space to list in this chapter.

17. The element of choice is beautifully expressed in an account by journalist Ron Rosenbaum of the lavish picnics on a private St Lawrence River island enjoyed by members of the exclusive Yale secret society, Skull and Bones: 'Of course, if the initiate has grown up in a Bones family and gone to picnics on the island all his life, the vision— the introduction to powerful people, the fine manners, the strong bonds—is less awesome. But to the non-hereditary slots in a Bones class of fifteen, the outsiders—frequently the football captain, the editor of the *Yale Daily News*, a brilliant scholar, a charismatic student politician—the island experience comes as a seductive revelation: these powerful people want me, want my talents, my services; perhaps they even want by genes. Play along with their rules and I can become one of them.' *Esquire*, September 1977.

18. Domhoff, pp. 73–5.

19. *Ibid.*, Chap. IV. esp. p. 110.

20. See pages 8–13.

21. In general see: Harold Perkin, *the Origins of Modern English Society* (1969); François Bédarida, *A Social History of England 1851–1975* (1979); F.M.L. Thompson, *English Landed Society in the Nineteenth Century* (1963); W.D. Rubinstein, 'Wealth, Elites and the Class Structure of Modern Britain', *Past and Present* (1977), pp. 99–126. My interpretation is not inconsistent with that recently presented by Lawrence Stone and J.C.F. Stone in *An Open Elite?: England 1540– 1880* (1984), save that for the twentieth century I see aristocracy, gentry, and other influential elements as together forming one extended upper class which has within it its own status distinctions.

22. Gathorne-Hardy. See also Robert Heussler, *Yesterday's Rulers: The Making of the British Colonial Service* (1963), pp. 86–7.

23. Cléo de Mérode, *Le Ballet de ma vie* (1955), p. 15.

24. In general see, Georges Dupeux, *French Society 1789–1970* (1972); A. Saury, *Histoire Economique* (1965–67); P. Chevallier, *L'Enseignement français de la revolution a nos jours*, 2 vols. (1968); John Ardagh, *The New France* (1970); John Blondel, *Contemporary France, Politics, Society and Institutions* (1974) M. Wurmser, 'Le Milieu administratif en France et a l'etranger', in *Institut technique des administrations publiques* (1951).

25. Gabriel A. Almond and Sidney Verba, *The Civic Culture: Political Attitudes and Democracy in Five Nations* (1963), p. 37. Reinhard Bendix, *Higher Civil Servants in American Society* (1949), p. 27.

26. American Federation of Labor Papers, US Mss., 117A/11C, box 3, Archives Division, The State Historical Society of Wisconsin, Madison.

27. See Leonard Silk and Mark Silk, *The American Establishment* (1980); Frederick Cople Jaher, *The Urban Establishment: Upper Strata in Boston, New York, Charleston, Chicago, and Los Angeles* (1982); Gabriel Kolko, 'Brahmins and Russians, 1870–1914: A Hypothesis on the Social Basis of Success in American History', in Kurt H. Wolff and Barrington Moore, Jr. (eds.), *The Critical Spirit* (1967), pp. 343–65.

See also C. David Heymann, *America's Aristocracy: The Lives and Times of James Russell, Amy and Robert Lowell* (1980). For the exclusive secret societies at Yale, see Ron Rosenbaum, 'An Elegy for Mumbo Jumbo', *Esquire*, September 1977.

28. Steven B. Levine, 'The Rise of American Boarding Schools and the Development of a National Upper Class', *Social Problems* (October 1980), pp. 63–94.

29. Maurice Halbwachs, *Les Classes sociales* (1942), p. 102.

30. Simon Raven, *The English Gentleman* (1964); Alan Churchill, *The Upper Crust* (1970); Mark Bence-Jones and Hugh Montgomery-Massingherd, *The British Aristocracy* (1979).

31. Denise François, 'Sur la variété des usages linguistiques chez les adultes: relations entre language et classes sociales', in *La Pensée* (1976), p. 66.

32. Arthur Marwick, *The Deluge: British Society and the First World War* (1965); *War and Social Change in the Twentieth Century* (1974), Ch. 3; *Britain in Our Century* (1984), Ch. 3, etc.

33. The classical statement was James Burnham, *The Managerial Revolution* (1940).

34. C. Wright Mills, *The Power Elite* (1956), 148; Maurice Zeitlin, 'Corporate Ownership and Control', *American Journal of Sociology*, vol. 79 (1974); Kolko, *op. cit.*, esp. p. 68; John Westergaard and Henrietta Resler, *Class in a Capitalist Society* (1975); P. Sargent Florence, *Ownership, Control and Success of Large Companies* (1961); Mabel Newcomer, *The Big Business Executive* (1965); W. Lloyd Warner and James Ableggan, *Big Business Leaders in America* (1963).

35. See Arthur Marwick, 'People's War and Top People's Peace?: British Society and the Second World War', in Alan Sked and Chris Cook (eds.) *Crisis and Controversy: Essays in Honour of A.J.P. Taylor* (1976), pp. 148–64; and *British Society Since 1945* (1982). David Cannadine, *Lords and Landlords: the Aristocracy and the Towns* (1980), pp. 425–9, gives a judicious account of the blows endured by the aristocracy *and* their remarkable post-war resilience.

36. Sir Ian Fraser to Miss Stanley, 11 May 1938, 'Class' Acc. No. 1420, BBC Written Archives, Caversham.

37. *Listener*, 13 October 1938.

38. A.L. Bowley, *Wages and Income in the United Kingdom since 1860* (1937); A.L. Bowley and Sir Josiah Stamp, *The National Income 1924* (1927); J.R. Hicks, *The Social Framework: an Introduction to Economics* (1942), p. 179; Josiah Wedgwood, *The Economics of Inheritance* (1929); A.M. Carr-Sauders and D. Caradog Jones, *A Survey of the Social Structure of England and Wales* (1927).

39 C.F.G. Masterman, *The Condition of England* (1909); *England After the War* (1922), Chs. II and III.

40. *England After the War*, p. 66.

41. H.W. Nevinson, *Running Accompaniments* (1936), p. 114.

42. *Ibid.*, pp. 120–1.

43. *Ibid.*, p. 124.

44. Edward Garnett, Introduction to *Letters from John Galsworthy 1900–1932* (1934), p. 6.
45. Margaret Newbolt (ed.), *The Life and Letters of Sir Henry Newbolt* (1942), *passim*.
46. Sir Henry Newbolt, *My World as in my Time: Memoirs* (1932), p. 48.
47. Robert Rhodes James (ed.), *Memoirs of a Conservative: J.C.C. Davidson's Memoirs and Papers, 1910–37* (1969), p. 103.
48. *Ibid.*, p. 5. Other information from *Dictionary of National Biography* and *Who was Who*.
49. *Memoirs of a Conservative*, p. 8.
50. Dalton Diaries, 20 May 1940, British Library of Political and Economic Science.
51. Crookshank Diaries, 20 July, 16 October 1934, 1 March, 6 October, 2 December 1935, Bodleian Library.
52. Dalton Diaries, *passim*.
53. John Strachey to Robert Boothby (n.d., 1928?), quoted in Hugh Thomas, *John Strachey* (1960), p. 65.
54. J.T. Murphy, *New Horizons* (1941), pp. 311–12; Ben Pimlott, *Labour and the Left in the 1930s* (1977), p. 180.
55. Cripps to Monckton, 28 December 1940, Monckton Papers, Bodleian Library.
56. Lord Londonderry to A. Beriedale Keith, 24 October 1940, A. Berriedale Keith Collection, GEN 145/4, University of Edinburgh Library; memo in Margesson Papers, 1/5, Churchill College, Cambridge; Neville Chamberlain to Leslie Scott, Lord Justice Scott papers, MSS119/3/P/CH, Modern Records Centre, University of Warwick.
57. See Bernard Crick, *George Orwell: A Life* (1980; revised edn. 1981), pp. 6–76 on which the rest of this paragraph is based.
58. Mary Agnes Hamilton, *Remembering my Good Friends* (1944), p. 37.
59. Lord Boyd Orr, *As I Recall* (1966), p. 149.
60. J.B. Priestley, *Margin Released* (1962), p. 4.
61. A.J. Cronin, *Adventures in Two Worlds* (1952), pp. 166–71.
62. *Ibid.*, pp. 173–4.
63. *Ibid.*, pp. 234–5.
64. Galsworthy to Garnett, 18 September 1910, Garnett *op. cit.*, p. 192.
65. John Galsworthy, *The Man of Property* (1951), in *The Forsyte Saga* (1922 collected edition), p. 3.
66. Galsworthy to Garnett, 18 September 1910, *loc. cit.*, p. 193.
67. *Ibid.*, 15 November 1910, *loc. cit.*, p. 197.
68. *The Forsyte Saga*, p. 766.
69. John Galsworthy, *A Modern Comedy* (1929), p. x.
70. Viscount Avon, Anthony Eden, *Another World 1897–1917* (1976); other information from DNB and *Who was Who*.
71. See Arthur Marwick, 'Middle Opinion in the Thirties', in *English Historical Review* (1964), pp. 285–98.
72. Harold Macmillan, *Winds of Change 1914–1939* (1966), p. 31.
73. *Ibid.*, p. 109.

74. R.K. Kelsall, *Higher Civil Servants in Britain* (1955), pp. 16 ff.
75. *DNB 1941–1950* (1959), p. 255.
76. Andrew Boyle, *Montagu Norman: A Biography* (1967), pp. 24, 8–24.
77. See Charlotte Erickson, *British Industrialists: Steel and Hosiery 1850–1950* (1959).
78. Charles Wilson, *A History of Unilever*, vol. I (1954), p. 200.
79. Erickson, *op. cit.*, p. 49.
80. J.M. Cohen, *The Life of Ludwig Mond* (1956), Chs. 5 and 6.
81. W.J. Reader, *Imperial Chemical Industries: A History*, vol. II (1975), Ch. 1.
82. Ian Fraser, *Whereas I was Blind* (1942), esp. pp. 7, 34.
83. See, e.g., *Revue d'économie politique*, vol. 53 (1939): *De la France d'avant guerre à la France d'aujourd'hui*, p. xv, 'l'ascension des classes populaires—le declin des classes bourgeoises'.
84. See, e.g., Jean Lhomme, *Le Problème des classes* (1938); Maurice Halbwachs, *Les Classes sociales* (1942), *Semaines Sociales de France*, XXXI, *Le Problème des Classes* (1942); and Louise-Marie Ferré, *Les Classes sociales dans la France contemporaine* (1934).
85. *Cours d'économie politique, professé en 1928–29 par M. François Simiand* (1929), pp. 440–85.
86. Gustave Moeder to Dollinger, 6 November 1932, Fonds Dollinger, Boite 2,2/11, Archives Municipales, Strasbourg.
87. Jougla de Morenas, *Noblesse 38* (1938), p. 8.
88. Association d'Entraide de la Noblesse Française, *Receuil des 'Personnes ayant fait leur preuves devant les Assemblées Générales, 1932–1949* (1950), preface by M. le duc de Lévis Mirepoix.
89. *Crapouillot*, March 1926, p. 17.
90. *Ibid.*, pp. 16–33.
91. Maurice Druon, *La Fin des hommes* (3 vols, 1948–51), vol. 1, p. 11, vol. 3, p. 9.
92. Vol. 3, pp. 279–80.
93. Jules Romains, *Les Hommes de bon volonté* (4 vol. edition, 1958), vol. IV, pp. 9 ff.
94. See Baumier, pp. 19 ff.
95. Romains, vol. IV, p. 325.
96. Jean Jolly, *Dictionaire des parlementaires français* (1960).
97. M. Dogan, 'L'Origine sociale du personnel parlementaire français', *Revue Français de Sociologie*, VIII (1967), p. 469; see also Jean Charlot, 'Les élites politiques en France de la IIIe à la Ve republique', *Archives Européennes de Sociologie*, XIV (1973).
98. Biographical information from Jolly, unless otherwise stated.
99. Louis Aubert *et al.*, *André Tardieu* (1957), Introduction.
100. Joseph Paul-Boncour, *Entre deux guerres: souvenirs de la IIIe République*, vol. I (1945).
101. Paul Reynaud, *Memoires* (1960), pp. 21–35.
102. *Ibid.*
103. See Henri Dubief, *Le Déclin de la IIIe République* (1976), p. 187.
104. *Crapouillot, loc. cit.*

105. Jean-Noël Jeanneney, *François de Wendel en république: l'argent et le pouvoir 1914–1940* (1975), pp. 612–14.
106. Alfred M. Bingham, *Insurgent America: Revolt of the Middle Classes* (1935), Lewis Corey, *The Crisis of the Middle Class* (1935). G.W. Hartman and T. Newcombe, (eds.), *Industrial Conflict* (1939); Arthur N. Holcombe, *The Middle Classes in American Politics* (1940); Franklin C. Palm, *The Middle Classes Then and Now* (1936); Selig Perelman, *A Theory of the Labor Movement* (1928); Helen and Robert Lynd, *Middletown* (1928); and *Middletown in Transition* (1937); W. Lloyd Warner and Paul S. Lunt, *The Status System of a Modern Community* (1942), A. Davis, B.B. Gardner and M.R. Gardner, *Deep South* (1941); and J. Dollard, *Class and Caste in a Southern Town* (1937).
107. E. Digby Baltzell, *Philadelphia Gentlemen: the Making of a National Upper Class* (1958), pp. 6–29.
108. McDuffie Collection, box 1, Atlanta University Library.
109. Dean Acheson, *Morning and Noon* (1965), pp. 164–5.
110. Friends of Franklin Roosevelt, *Franklin D. Roosevelt: Who He Is and . . . What He has Done* (1932); 'The Boy with the Gold Spoon', *Tulsa Tribune*, September 18, 1932 (Moley Collection, Hoover Institution).
111. *The Secret Diary of Harry L. Ickes* (1955) vol. 3, pp. 318–19.
112. Quoted by R.J. Whalen, *The Founding Father: The Story of Joseph P. Kennedy* (1965, paperback edition 1976), p. 32.
113. *Ibid.*, p. 3.
114. John Dos Passos, *USA* (1983 collected edition), p. 260.
115. *Ibid.*, p. 113.
116. Malcolm Cowley, Introduction to *Three Novels of Scott Fitzgerald* (1953), p. xvi. F. Scott Fitzgerald, *The Great Gatsby* (1963).
117. Suzanne Keller, *The Social Origins and Career Lines of Three Generations of American Business Leaders* (1953; 1980 reprint), p. 36.
118. Edward Pessen, *Log Cabin Myths: The Social Background of the Presidents* (1984), pp. 172, 154.
119. Biographical information from *Who was Who in America*.
120. G. William Domhoff, *Who Rules America?* (1967), and *The Higher Circles: The Governing Class in America* (1970); John N. Ingham, *The Iron Barons: A Social Analysis of the American Urban Elite* (1978); Kolko, *Wealth and Power*.
121. Richard P. Coleman and Lee Rainwater, *Social Standing in America: New Dimensions of Class* (1978), p. 26.
122. Alison Davis, *Psychology of the Child in the Middle Class* (1960), pp. 4–5.
123. *Life*, 21 March 1960; *New York Times*, 19 November 1980, p. B2.
124. Helen Van Slyke, *Public Smiles, Private Tears* (1982, paperback edition 1983), pp. 18–19.
125. Judith Krantz, *Scruples* (1978, paperback edition 1979), pp. 10–11.
126. *San Francisco Sunday Examiner and Chronicle*, November 4, 1984.
127. Pierre Laroque, *Les grands problèmes sociaux contemporains* (1954–55), p. 71.
128. *Ibid.*, pp. 71–143.

129. Pierre Birnbaum, *op. cit.*; Jean Baumier, *op. cit.*; Olgierd Lewandowski, 'Differenciation et mécanismes d'intégration de la classe dirigeante', *Economie et Statistique* (1970); Ezra. N. Suleiman, *Elites in French Society* (1978); and Bertrand Bellon, *Le Pouvoir financier et l'industrie en France* (1980). See also Gérard Vincent, *Les Français 1945–1975: chronologie et structure d'une societé* (1977), 352 ff.
130. François de Negroni, *La France Noble* (1974), pp. 17–18.
131. *Ibid.*, pp. 20–1.
132. *Ibid.*, pp. 29–33.
133. Baumier, p. 134.
134. *Ibid.*, p. 108.
135. *Ibid.*, p. 144.
136. Dossier on *Les Amants* at Cinematèque de Toulouse.
137. Dudley Seers, *The Levelling of Incomes since 1938* (1951), p. 10; Ivan Reid, *Social Class Differences in Britain* (1977).
138. Anthony Crosland, *The Future of Socialism* (1956).
139. Benwell Community Project, *The Making of a Ruling Class* (1978).
140. John Fidler, *The British Business Elite: Its Attitudes to Class, Status and Power* (1981), Ch. 7.
141. *Ibid.*, p. 181.
142. Mark Bence-Jones and Hugh Montgomery-Massingherd, *The British Aristocracy* (1979), p. 2.
143. *Ibid.*, p. 156.
144. Arthur Marwick, *Class: Image and Reality in Britain, France and the USA since 1930* (1980), Ch. 16. The bibliography of this book, p. 377–400 provides a more complete list of sources for the issues raised in this chapter than there is room for here.
145. Arthur Marwick, *British Society since 1945*, pp. 214–17.
146. *Who's Who in France.*
147. Shoup, pp. 15–17.
148. Anthony Giddens, *The Class Structure of the Advanced Societies* (1973, 1981 edition), p. 107.

CHAPTER THREE

Class, Estate and Status in the Czech Lands, 1919–1938

Maggie Smales

With the exception of contemporary Russia, one would probably search in vain for a society as unified and democratically homogeneous as that of the Czechs.[1]

(Jaromir John, novelist and journalist, 1933)

The notion that the Czechs of the inter-war period were a socially homogeneous people was a commonplace amongst contemporary non-Marxist observers and has been echoed by western historians. A mythology has developed around the idea of Czechoslovakia, and especially the Czech Lands, as the 'classic country of the little man', distracting attention from both the burgeoning Czech political and economic bourgeoisie and the large, impoverished industrial and agricultural proletariat. For Marxist commentators the existence of these two extremes itself embodied the essential truth about the nature of inter-war Czech society, and the stark class conflict pictured by early Communist Party Congresses has become the bedrock of more recent analysis.[2]

In this chapter I shall use the empirical methods of historical research described in the Introduction to look beyond the political rhetoric of these conflicting claims. By examining the 'historical context', I shall identify the salient features of economic and political development which helped to shape Czech* society, for the Czech Lands did not present a classic picture of modern urban industrial society, and the First World

---

*The German population of the Czech Lands has been excluded from the scope of this enquiry.

War and the establishment of a new state had their own impact on social divisions and attitudes. I shall then bring together contemporary sources ranging from the legal and bureaucratic to the anecdotal to illustrate certain common assumptions about class and about other dimensions of stratification within Czech society. Finally I shall examine demonstrable facts of social inequality such as the distribution of wealth and the nature of housing. The integration of this 'subjective' and 'objective' evidence will lead to general conclusions about the nature and historical import of class in the Czech Lands in the period 1918–38.

The Historical Context

Ostensibly, the provinces of Bohemia and Moravia-Silesia* had already achieved the economic profile of a modern industrial society by the time of independence. The first post-war census, dating from 1921, showed that, in Bohemia, 40.55 per cent of the population was engaged in industry and handicrafts, and only 29.69 per cent in agriculture, forestry and fishing. The figures for Moravia-Silesia were 37.79 per cent and 35.27 per cent, respectively. The gap between industry and agriculture widened still further in the following decade. By 1930 only 24.06 per cent of Bohemia's workers were employed in agriculture, in comparison to 41.78 per cent in industry, whilst Moravia had experienced the fastest industrial development in the Republic, with 40.82 per cent of the population now engaged in industry, and a much diminished 28.56 per cent in agriculture.[3] The proportion of the industrial population in the Czech Lands, taken as a whole, was about equal to that in Germany and was, in Europe, exceeded only by Great Britain, Belgium, the Netherlands and Switzerland.[4]

Yet in 1937 a British observer was able to describe Bohemia as 'a country . . . with few of the phenomena of modern industrialisation'.[5] It is crucial to the understanding of Czech social attitudes in the inter-war period to realise that this

---

*The province of Silesia was merged with Moravia for administrative purposes in 1927. The term Moravia can be taken to imply both Moravia and Silesia.

apparently advanced capitalist society in fact retained many characteristics of pre-industrial times.

Social development had been affected by the tempo of industrialisation in the Czech Lands. Progress was hampered by the inertia of what was still a semi-feudal state—labour service was not abolished until 1848 and the guild system survived until 1859. Rapid industrialisation finally got underway in mid-century, but the period of prosperity came to an abrupt end with the financial crash of 1873 and there followed several years of industrial crisis. The shock of this economic collapse served to reinforce the anti-capitalist instincts of a traditional society. Whatever the truth in their complaints, Czech businessmen and financiers were to bemoan the lack of capitalist spirit amongst their compatriots right up to the Second World War.[6]

Economic growth began to rise again around 1880, but it was not until the mid-1890s that rapid industrial development once more set in, and the two decades before the First World War mark the real apogee of the industrial revolution in the Czech Lands. Thus, in 1918, many members of the Czech industrial proletariat were only one or two generations removed from the land, and they often still maintained family connections with their native villages. Similarly, few families amongst the Czech economic bourgeoisie had been entrepreneurs for more than two generations. These were factors of crucial importance for the self-image of Czech society as the society of the 'little man'.

Despite the considerable progress of industrialisation, a very large percentage of the population continued, throughout the inter-war period, to live in villages and small towns. The 1930 census showed that 31.5 per cent of the Bohemian population and 49.6 per cent of the population of Moravia-Silesia lived in communities of less than 2000 persons; in Germany, in 1925, the comparable figure was 35.6 per cent.[7] Indeed, a high proportion of the industrial population of the Czech Lands were resident in rural or semi-rural communities. The coalminer or the engineering worker who combined industrial employment with labour on his family's smallholding was a common figure, and these so-called metal-agriculturalists (kovozemědělci) cannot be classified unambiguously as members of an industrial proletariat. Moreover, the proportion of the population actually employed in agriculture was still sufficient, at 25.6 per cent, to constitute a substantial peasant class.

Another crucial factor in assessing the nature of Czech social structure is the size of industrial concerns. The industrial census of 1930 suggests a society in which small-scale production and craftwork continued to be extremely important. Of all the people employed in industry and handicrafts in that year, 34.7 per cent worked in small concerns with less than six employees, and only six factories in the Czech Lands had more than 5000 employees.[8] Someone classed as an industrial worker according to the 1930 population census might, therefore, be one of the 26,000 employees of the Skoda engineering works, and live in Plzen, an industrial city with a population of 114,000. He might equally well be the only employee of a craft workshop in a village.

The particular combination of progressiveness and retardation which characterised economic life in the Czech Lands was also apparent in industrial relations. Czechoslovakia was one of the most highly unionised countries in the world, ranking fourth in 1928 with 12.3 per cent of the total population being union members.[9] However, despite its apparent numerical strength, the trades union movement was highly fragmented. Every major political party, including the German parties, had its own union movement and there were separate federations for white-collar employees and university graduates. The labour movement was much weakened by these ethnic and political divisions and, in addition, most individual unions were craft-based, rather than covering whole industries.[10]

Culturally and socially, Czech society in 1918 was essentially provincial. Until independence the Czech Lands were part of a much larger whole, and Prague, although the focus of Czech culture and the second banking sity in the Empire, could not be claimed as a city of European or world significance. Much of the industry in the Czech Lands was controlled by Viennese interests, and thousands of Czechs sought a living in the Imperial capital. High society was oriented towards Vienna and at the top of the social pyramid stood the Imperial Court, the aristocracy, the high bureaucracy, the diplomatic corps, the higher-ranking clergy and the officer corps. Very few Czechs ever penetrated into these exclusive circles.[11]

In 1918 the Czechoslovak Republic needed a government, an administrative apparatus, a diplomatic service and an army. There was a sudden expansion of career opportunities which brought considerable social mobility for some citizens of the new state. The new ministries in Prague were staffed in part by Czech bureaucrats from Vienna. Other recruits came from the provincial bureaucracies. National prejudice, and later language ordinances, hindered many of the Germans formerly employed from working in government service and there were few suitably qualified Slovaks. Similar factors operated in recruitment to the other state services. In the army, for example, preferment went initially to ex-legionaries who were, by definition, mainly Czechs.[12]

Czech businessmen also benefited from independence. In the uncertain political atmosphere after the end of the war, Czech banks were able to buy up shares in firms which had previously been controlled by German capital. Moreover 'nostrification' ensured that every concern operating on Czechoslovak territory had to have its head office in the Republic and appoint a majority of Czechoslovak citizens to its Board of Directors.[13] Thus the rise of the new state had a profound impact on the distribution of power and wealth, strengthening and expanding the upper strata of Czech society at the expense of the once dominant Germans.

In the expansion of career opportunities of all kinds which followed independence, education took on a particular significance as a means to social mobility. Traditionally a source of great prestige, the winning of formal educational qualifications was also a necessary preliminary to many sought-after careers, including state service and membership of the so-called 'free professions'. Indeed, of the 80 inter-war Czech government ministers, no fewer than 37 were doctors of law and many of the rest had a university qualification of some kind.[14] The system which had been inherited from the Habsburgs gave a basic state education to pupils from all backgrounds. However, the rigidity and highly stratified nature of the educational system was often a barrier to the talented children of the lower social strata—only about 5 per cent of children went on to grammar school at the age of eleven, and most of them came from the families of salaried employees.[15] Even fewer actually left school with the *maturita* (matriculation certificate) which allowed entry to university, whilst the majority of pupils spent the whole of their compulsory education in an elementary school and gained no formal qualifications. The first President of the Republic may have been the son of a coachman, but a survey of secondary school graduates in the Czech Lands undertaken in 1933–34 suggested that, in general, 'upward social mobility does not take place in a single social leap, but rather in successive short steps'.[16]

In the heightened atmosphere of the first months of independence, much lip-service was paid to the need for what Karel Engliš, later to become Minister of Finance, called, 'not just adjustments, but radical changes to the social order'.[17] The Czechs at last had the opportunity to translate into practical terms the democratic ideology of their nineteenth-century nationalist leaders, and social unrest in the aftermath of four years of war made some action imperative. Social stabilisation was helped by a series of legislative measures, starting with the introduction of an eight-hour working day in December 1918. Unemployment benefits were introduced and social insurance of all kinds was gradually extended and improved. For the first time agricultural labourers were included within the provision of social legislation and their contracts of employment were placed on the same legal basis as those of industrial workers— an important point in any mapping of the Czech social order in the inter-war years. Land reform strengthened the position of the small and medium peasant farmer, whilst at the same time undermining the position of the largely German nobility. However, these were in essence conservative reforms, which did not alter existing social structures in a fundamental way. Rather, they improved the quality of life for manual workers and peasants, ensuring their basic loyalty to the new state.[18]

As well as distinctions based on economic factors, or education, there were alternative focuses of social identification for the Czechs of the inter-war period. Religion, for example, could act as a unifying factor across social barriers, although it was somewhat less potent a force in the Czech Lands than in Slovakia. At the inception of the Republic many Czechs still identified the Catholic Church with German political and cultural domination and the ultra-conservative Habsburg establishment, and over 1¼ million of them renounced their Catholic faith after independence. Of these, half a million joined the reformist, anti-papal Czechoslovak Church, but over 640,000 people in Bohemia and 55,000 in Moravia now declared themselves to be 'without confession'. None the less, Catholicism continued to be important in rural areas, and it maintained a position of dominance in Moravia, where the Populist Party consistently won the largest share of the vote in the inter-war parliamentary elections.[19]

Once the Czechs were freed from the immediate threat of Sudeten German intransigence, nationalism was no longer as strong a motivating force as it had been before 1918. Independence fulfilled many of their socio-economic aspirations, and they were very much the dominant nation of the Republic. Nevertheless, nationalism lingered below the surface to emerge in times of stress. Hitler's success in the September 1930 elections in Germany, for example, was very closely followed by four days of anti-German riots in Prague.[20] Moreover, the claims of nationalism could be used to disguise what were essentially class issues, as in 1930, when there was considerable opposition to government plans to increase emergency payments to the unemployed because the worst-hit areas were German-inhabited.[21] As a positive force, too, nationalism could always unite Czech society in the face of external threat; this was especially apparent in 1938.

Karel Čapek wrote of the birth of the Czechoslovak Republic in October 1918: 'We felt as if we had stepped into a paradise in which everything would be better. It seemed as if the Age of Justice had dawned, as if the social order had changed of its own accord . . . .'.[22] Nineteenth-century nationalist ideology had encouraged in the Czechs a strong sense of democratic mission, a belief that they were called upon to transform society, and create something uniquely their own. Yet the first act of the Provisional Government was essentially pragmatic, declaring that all existing provincial and imperial laws should remain in force. The interaction between democratic ideology and the Habsburg inheritance did much to shape class perceptions in the inter-war years. Belief in egalitarianism coexisted with a deeply ingrained sense of social hierarchy. The republican citizen had, until 1918, been the loyal subject of the Emperor Franz Joseph, and whatever the democratic aspirations of the new age, the social attitudes left by rank-conscious Habsburg society were hard to eradicate.

The Images

The first category of materials to be examined includes the census, Acts of Parliament and documents relating to social policy: in other words sources which emanated from various government departments and other official agencies during the inter-war period. These legal and bureaucratic sources will be analysed to reveal official perceptions of the broad social divisions within Czech society. Although the 1920 constitution guaranteed citizens equality before the law, stressing that 'privileges relating to sex, birth or profession will not be recognised', it is clear that certain fundamental distinctions, notably the manual/non-manual divide, were underpinned by law.[23] Official pronouncements often provided an institutionalised basis for social boundaries, as well as illustrating the nature of social prejudice at this time.

The census is the only official source which presented a detailed scheme for the breakdown of society into various groups and sub-groups. The actual categories used in inter-war Czechoslovakia were taken over, with only slight modifications, from a classification scheme devised by the Austrian Bureau of Statistics in 1890, in order to reflect the change which the industrial revolution had brought to the economic profile of society. The degree of socio-economic continuity was obviously sufficient for this to be regarded as an appropriate analytical tool even after independence.

Most revealing as a statement on the nature of social stratification was the census's categorisation of 'occupational standing'. Initially six horizontal divisions were recognised: the self-employed, tenants, officials, workers, apprentices and day labourers—the order suggesting an implicit hierarchy. Some of these divisions were less clear-cut than others; the 'self-employed' included many members of the economic bourgeoisie and practitioners of the liberal professions, but also market traders and hot-chestnut sellers; 'officials' might be civil servants or school teachers, but also top managers in industry. Predictably, present-day Czech historians claim this as an attempt to disguise the class structure of inter-war society.[24] Yet the census does disclose some of the main social preoccupations of that period.

Most important of all, the census helped to define the distinction between manual and non-manual labour. The first census in the independent Republic, held in 1921, placed this crucial divide between the categories 'officials' and 'workers'. However, this decision came under immediate criticism as a simplification of social reality.[25] In 1930 an intermediate category was created for *'zřízenci'* (lower-ranking, non-manual employees). Explanatory notes to the census claimed that the growth of mass production and the expansion of service industries meant that there was an increasing number of specialist and supervisory jobs which brought their practitioners higher wages and greater job security than ordinary manual workers. These specialist workers were said to form a new social stratum, acutely aware of the social differentiation between themselves and their manual counterparts.[26] Like officials, *zřízenci* were in receipt of the superior state pension insurance provided for white-collar workers. In disputed cases, the kind of social insurance received was indeed the decisive factor in clarifying 'occupational standing'.[27]

The census also described officially perceived divisions within the manual working class—'workers', 'apprentices' and 'day labourers' in the 1921 version, with an additional category for 'home workers' added in 1930. The separate classification of apprentices is a reminder that the guild system was not abolished until 1859, and that formal training as an apprentice was still, in the inter-war years, a necessary prerequisite for a very wide range of occupations. Homeworkers, who occupied an uneasy position between the self-employed and wage labour, were especially numerous in the German border areas; the fact of their existence as a significant group recalls the traditional nature of much industry in the Czech Lands. The distinction made between 'workers' and 'day labourers' is significant, although the terminology used was confusing. In practice, skilled workers were classed as 'workers' even if paid by the day. 'Day labourers' comprised unskilled workers in industry and trade, seasonal workers in agriculture, irrespective of their level of skill, and any other casual labourers: the obvious implication was that they were of lower social status.[28] Thus the census suggested a somewhat diverse working class, with a potential 'under class' of unskilled and casual labour, and a non-manual work force ('officials' and '*zřízenci*') divided according to level of skill and education, but failed to locate the economic bourgeoisie.

A more rewarding area than the census for the study of official perceptions of class is to be found in certain aspects of social and employment legislation. The tendency for such legislation to institutionalise basic social divisions was hardly confined to Czechoslovakia; in France, for example, the *Code du Travail* reflected the 'distinction between the intellectual and non-intellectual qualities of the white-collar and manual workers respectively', a distinction also enshrined in present-day German social insurance.[29] The legislative distinction made between manual and non-manual labour in inter-war Czechoslovakia was actually a leftover from Habsburg times. In Cisleithania, social and employment legislation had recognised four distinct categories of workers: manual workers, miners, white-collar employees and government employees. The separate provisions made for miners and government employees were, by 1918, something of an historical anachronism, a reflection of the lingering influence of the social ranks and orders of estate society. More important was the recognition of a broad societal divide between manual and non-manual workers, which reflected implicit assumptions about the different needs and rights of the two basic kinds of labour.

At the inception of the new Republic, in the prevailing spirit of radical democracy, it seemed possible that a new uniform approach to employment legislation might be possible. The eight-hour day, enacted in December 1918, applied to both manual and non-manual workers alike, and compulsory sickness insurance was extended to all categories of employees the following year. However, when a committee of the National Assembly was set up to discuss the creation of an 'all-national agency for general social insurance' the forces of establishment were quick to respond. Social attitudes were too deeply ingrained, and existing institutions too deeply entrenched, for the kind of sweeping change initially envisaged. The committee of enquiry was inundated by hundreds of letters and petitions seeking to influence its deliberations against such a decision.[30]

It is hardly surprising, therefore, that manual workers were eventually awarded separate and less extensive social benefits than those enjoyed by white-collar employees. Dr Evžen Štern, one of the Social Democratic Party's leading experts on social policy, claimed that legislation for the latter was based on the idea that 'the transition from active service to pension should not mean a complete reversal in the economic life of the person insured', whereas manual workers' insurance was intended simply to remove 'the undeserved blackest poverty, which can hurl the individual worker, or even a whole family, into physical and moral poverty'.[31] Manual workers received an old-age pension at 65, irrespective of sex, whereas white-collar employees retired at 60 if male and 55 if female. The basic pension guaranteed by law was 500 crowns a year for manual workers, whilst white-collar employees were entitled to a minimum of 3600 crowns. The widows of white-collar employees received pensions automatically, whereas workers' widows had a right to a pension only if they were over 65, or invalids, or had the care of two or more children under the age of 17.[32] When this particular provision was discussed in committee, the opinion was expressed that workers' wives were used to working to earn their own living, and often did so during their husbands' lifetimes, so they required no special provision for widowhood.[33] All of these provisions reflect a very great qualitative difference in the perceived needs of manual workers and white-collar employees, and of their appropriate social station.

The concept of invalidity, too, was vastly different for manual workers and white-collar employees. For the latter, invalidity signified professional invalidity, or the inability to pursue one's own particular profession. Workers, however, even if skilled in a particular trade, were not allowed to claim a pension automatically when illness prevented them from pursuing it. They only received a pension if their earning capacity was reduced by two-thirds, which for most meant, in effect, if they were reduced to beggary. In denying to manual workers that professional particularism which it accepted as a natural right amongst salaried employees, the law underlined the overriding importance of their common identity as workers.

Given the great difference in social provisions for the two types of labour, it was obviously very important for the legislators to delimit precisely the division between manual and mental work. This proved a difficult task. The Pensions Act of 1920 was intended to apply to 'employees who primarily undertake mental work, or who regularly oversee the work of others' and to exclude those whose work was of a 'subordinate nature'.[34] The interpretation of these phrases led to numerous disputed cases. Was a chauffeur, for example, a 'mentally active' worker because his job required a certain amount of technical knowledge, driving skill and presence of mind? Not according to the High Court, which claimed that driving a car, repairing it and keeping it in good working order required no special mental powers.[35] On the other hand, an assistant in a stationer's shop was declared eligible for pension insurance as her responsibilities required 'knowledge, training and alacrity', even though the prices were already marked on the goods which she sold.[36] The main difference here would appear to lie not in the actual level of skill, but in whether a job required the employee to dirty his hands occasionally. In the revised Pensions Act of 1929, it was found desirable to enumerate in minute detail the specific professions which were felt to be deserving of superior insurance benefits, and which were categorised, tellingly, as a 'higher form of service' (vyšší služba).[37]

As well as underpinning the distinction between the two basic kinds of labour, social and employment legislation also gave rise to a second, and far less clearly articulated, social divide. Certain categories of workers, like seasonal labourers in agriculture or servants, were often excluded from the provisions of such legislation. The scope of each measure was different, and some were more all-embracing than others, so it is difficult to piece together an unambiguous picture of an officially-perceived 'underclass'. None the less, there was a certain suggestion that some people were felt to be undeserving, for whatever reason, of the level of social protection afforded to the majority of the population. The legislation for an eight-hour day, for example, did not apply to servants or agricultural workers who lived in; accident insurance did not extend to agricultural labourers; unemployment benefits were limited to union members (which in practice tended to mean skilled workers and white-collar workers). The underprivileged status of unskilled and casual labour was thereby reinforced.[38]

Although official sources do not make explicit reference to 'class', they do set out a basic hierarchy, implicitly tied to a concept of social merit. The working class was divided between the skilled and the unskilled; the former were afforded comprehensive, if basic, social protection by the state, the latter were largely left to fend for themselves. Between manual and non-manual labour was a further divide, and the very fact that the latter was officially labelled 'service of a higher nature', and rewarded as such, encapsulated the social prejudices of the time. There was another, less fundamental, distinction based on job prestige (and indirectly on level of education) between 'officials' and the lower-ranking *zřízenci*, and the census terms provide labels for social stereotypes which will recur throughout this chapter. As in other countries, the upper echelons of society escaped official observations.[39]

If official sources reveal a broad framework of social analysis, the programmes of the main political parties add more intimate detail. Seven parties dominated the electoral scene in Czech-inhabited areas—the Agrarian Party, the National Democratic Party, the Populist Party, the Small Tradesmen's Party, the National Socialist Party, the Social Democratic Party and the Communist Party. The first six, at one time or another, took part in the various coalition governments of the inter-war period. Each had an explicit party programme, although ideology tended to be relatively unchanging. There were only two major programme revisions in the inter-war years, undertaken by the Social Democrats in 1930 and the National Socialists in 1931, and some party programmes had altered little since pre-war times. Whatever the day-to-day response to changing political and economic circumstances, the perceptions of broad social divisions and the social stereotypes used remained somewhat static. The Communist Party, an important force of opposition, relied for its programme on the tenets of Marx and Lenin, as interpreted by the Third International. In so far as it developed a response to specific Czech conditions, this is revealed in the proceedings of the various inter-war party congresses.[40]

A common characteristic of the parties under consideration was their preoccupation with Marxist theories of class. Of course, the Social Democratic Party and the Communist Party had avowedly Marxist origins, but all the other parties, without exception, felt compelled to take up a stance towards Marxism. The Marxist concept of class war, in particular, was seen as a very real threat to social stability and as such to be either modified or denied in each of the non-Marxist parties' schematic accounts of how society functioned. No party really questioned the issue of whether classes could be said to exist, although some parties stated very clearly that classes ought not to exist, appealing to a higher, unifying factor such as 'the common good of the nation and the state', which they felt should override such narrow sectional interests.[41]

Despite obvious differences of opinion about the nature and historical importance of social divisions, the parties did offer broadly similar opinions about the most significant groupings in Czech society. Reference to four professional categories—agriculturalists, tradesmen, officials and lower-ranking white collar workers (*zřízenci*) and workers—occur in a more or less systematic fashion throughout political pronouncements of this period. Indeed, to certain of the political parties, three of these groups represented a kind of redeeming force for the whole of society. The Agrarian Party, or to give it its full title, the Republican Party of Agricultural and Small Farming People, saw the agricultural population fulfilling such a role. The Tradesmen's and Shopkeepers Party of the Middle Estate and the Social Democratic Workers' Party each stressed the crucial importance of the social groups out of which they had arisen. The Communists' idealisation of the 'revolutionary' working class was a similar case.

In so far as the various parties did put forward policies relating to the agricultural population, they were agreed in treating those people who worked on the land as a separate community. Both the Populists and the National Democrats, for example, recognised the existence of an agricultural 'estate'. Although the official ideologies of the three socialist parties stressed the common interests of the lower strata of both rural and urban society, their pronouncements, however unwittingly, do suggest that the agricultural population had to be treated as a distinct entity. The Communist Party, in particular, was perennially preoccupied with the 'Agrarian Question'. The Agrarians, self-styled representatives of 'agricultural and small farming people', made the slogan 'the village is one family' a salient feature of their political ideology, claiming a mystical 'law of the land' which united 'all who live on the land . . . by a bond far stronger than divisions of property, religion or profession'. Agrarian democracy was said to acknowledge 'no differences according to cut of coat or size of landholding; it recognises only equal members of a party who . . . are united by the same estate interests'.[42]

The socialist parties, in contrast, sought rather to stress socio-economic divisions within rural society and to highlight, in particular, the lack of social and economic rights amongst small farmers and agricultural labourers. The Communists, for example, poured scorn on the Agrarian claim that 'everyone from the agricultural labourer and the dwarf-holder to Mr Schwarzenberg and Sonntág, President of the Anglobanka is [a member] of one family'. They preferred rather to divide the agricultural population between the 'exploited and the oppressed' and the 'exploiters of labour'; even contrasting the lives of small farmers' wives, worn out by work and financial worries, with the good fortune of estate owners' and rich peasants' wives who did not have to work and looked 'as if they were made of butter'.[43] The National Socialists and the Social Democrats both emphasised the need for a new land reform to help small owners. The former went so far as to suggest that the original reform of 1919 had served the interests of a 'restricted caste of richer farmers' and had, in effect, created a new landed gentry (*zemanstvo*). The Social Democrats were also concerned to improve the working conditions of farm labourers and to abolish the legal code of practice covering such workers, the *čeledni řád*, which still contained such anachronistic provisions as a ban on luxurious clothing.[44]

However, despite such appeals to sectional interest in the

farming community, the socialist parties had to admit that agriculture's lower strata often supported the Agrarians for 'reasons of estate consciousness', even though that movement did not necessarily meet their social needs.[45] The Agrarian Party had a very powerful weapon in its idealisation of the peasant, who was encouraged to think of himself as 'the most creative element in the state . . . a source of regeneration for the nation . . .'.[46] Such sentiments fed on prejudices shared by many sectors of the agricultural community, irrespective of any social or economic hierarchy. They also encouraged a certain resentment of industry and the towns, which heightened the agricultural community's sense of separate identity.

The second social group distinguished in the party programmes comprised the various categories of small businessmen for whom the Tradesmen's and Shopkeepers' Party of the Middle Estate claimed to be the main political representative. The non-socialist parties were at one in regarding this group as a bastion of the social order. Populist ideology, for instance, expressed sentimental attachment to the notion of the small businessman who was 'neither too rich nor too poor', and whose independence saved him from 'the psychosis of the mob'. The tradesmen's own party claimed that its constituents formed 'the basis of economic independence for both the individual and the nation'. For the socialist parties, of course, the concentration of capital and the decline of the small business was part of the natural progression of history. They hoped to enlist the small businessman as an ally of, rather than a model for, the working class in the struggle for a more just society.[47]

The action programmes of the various parties reveal something of the economic and social standing of shopkeepers and tradesmen. There was, for instance, a general demand to extend pension legislation to the self-employed, which underlined the vulnerability of the small businessman who was not covered by such welfare benefits. The non-socialist parties were also concerned—at least in theory—to bolster up the somewhat precarious financial position of many small businesses; indeed the Populists and the Tradesmen's Party wanted to mount a full-scale attack on capitalism.[48] There is a strong sense of nostalgia here for pre-industrial society, and the protection once afforded to small producers by the guild system. Yet despite a tendency to idealise the small businessman, the Tradesmen's Party was very defensive about the actual social standing of its members, and even found it necessary to call for schoolchildren to be 'inculcated with a desire for economic independence and a love of craft work'.[49] In fact, the overall impression gained from the party programmes is of a group beleaguered on all sides by economic insecurity and lack of social estimation.

The third social group, comprising officials, teachers and lower-ranking white-collar workers (*zřízenci*), was perhaps the most amorphous of all the divisions of Czech society described in the party programmes. The disparate nature of this group is illustrated by the fact that it had no specific party of its own. Indeed, only the National Democrats and the Populists devoted separate sections of their programmes to what they both saw as one of the four 'estates' in Czech society. Both parties placed great emphasis on the distinction between manual and non-manual work, claiming that this group of white-collar employees 'can be distinguished from [manual] workers by their training, the character of their work, their greater job security and their higher pay'.[50] In stressing that *zřízenci*, too, were to be considered as non-manual employees and, therefore, as a distinct social category from workers, the two parties followed a precedent set in both employment legislation and later the census.

The socialist parties, in contrast, sought to stress that all categories of labour, both manual and non-manual, shared common interests in the struggle against capital. Both the National Socialists and the Social Democrats pointed to the hardship suffered by salaried employees during the First World War, and suggested that they had been radicalised and, indeed, proletarianised by their experiences.[51] Certainly, complaints of financial hardship were common, and the Populist Party, in 1920, claimed significantly that even 'the lowest placed official' should receive a decent living wage.[52] However, most salaried employees, whatever their financial circumstances, remained conscious of their separate status. Many of them, in practice, identified with the idea of belonging to an intelligentsia, which led both the Tradesmen's and the Agrarian Parties to condemn 'the exaggerated elevation of mental workers to the status of an intelligentsia' because the formal absolution of school education 'does not always ennoble the spirit'.[53] It was, of course, unusual for either small farmers or small businessmen to complete the *maturita* (school-leaving certificate) which was the basic qualification for both teachers and officials. Hence these two parties' concern that trade and agriculture should not be underestimated socially in comparison to those professions which did require a certain educational standard.

Despite the desire of the non-socialist parties to suggest a certain social unity between peasants, small businessmen and salaried employees, they all succumbed to the temptation to deal with the three groups separately in their political programmes. References to the concept of a 'middle estate' (*střední stav*) bore the mark of political rhetoric, and it was usually found necessary to enumerate just which social groups were included in this description. In contrast, all the parties readily identified some kind of working class, although most preferred to use the more neutral term *dělnictvo* (the manual workforce). This is not to say that the parties regarded labour as absolutely monolithic. There was some suggestion of a divide betwen agricultural labourers and the industrial proletariat, based as much on attitudes as material interests.[54] The Communist Party, moreover, distinguished an 'aristocracy' of well-paid workers, 'a foreign body in the working class', who were said to be encouraged by the bourgeoisie to undermine solidarity, and were, by implication, Social Democratic voters. It also sought to identify the most militantly class-conscious sector of the working class, and spoke first of recruiting young, unskilled workers in large concerns, especially those who had been recently enlisted in the production process, and later the unemployed.[55] These distinctions are important, for they give the impression that although most manual workers felt a common social identity, only a minority were likely to seek change through revolution.

The picture of working-class life which emerges from the party programmes is one of considerable insecurity and material hardship. The Social Democrats, for example, sought to gain improvements in the social benefits received by workers and their families, castigating existing provisions as 'a superior form of poor relief'.[56] The Populists drew attention to the unsatisfactory condition of much working-class housing, stating that there should be a ban on cellar and basement dwellings, and that adequate drainage, healthy water supplies and proper refuse disposal should be provided.[57] There was, moreover, general agreement that the working class, more than any other section of society, was subject to fluctuations in the economy which could lead to sudden unemployment. Although there was some suggestion of improvement since independence, in particular in the growing extent of collective bargaining and in the effects of those social benefits already introduced, however limited their scope, most parties saw far-reaching change as necessary to bring about substantive improvement in the manual worker's lot. They were less willing to take concrete action to realise these intentions.

It is a noticeable feature of the various party programmes that they were concerned almost exclusively with the interests of what the National Socialists called 'small and middling people'. There was no clear concept of an upper stratum or strata, apart from almost ritual remarks about the evils of capital: even the National Democrats spoke of 'the voracity of big business'.[58] The two traditional sectors of society, the peasant community and small businessmen and artisans, were regarded with much sentimental attachment, although it is clear that, in practice, these occupations were rewarded with a somewhat low social status. Such attitudes suggested a society which had not yet come to terms with the reality of extensive industrialisation. There seems to have been a fairly fundamental division between the peasantry and urban society and a further crucial distinction between manual and non-manual labour. At the bottom of the social hierarchy was a working class for which social legislation had to a certain extent created a common legal identity, but which was far from homogeneous and was not, on the whole, militantly class-conscious.

The picture of social stratification built up from examination of the various parties' political programmes can be further illuminated by reference to a range of academic writings on the nature of class, the structure of society and the character of individual social groups. The qualification 'academic' has been used to exclude purely journalistic accounts of society (which are cited rather as 'informal perceptions' later in this chapter) and those political polemics which can be seen simply as an extension of party ideology.

'Class' *per se* was never a major preoccupation of inter-war scholarly writers. The word itself was perhaps too emotive, too closely associated with Marxist doctrine, to encourage non-polemical debate. Indeed, one of the encyclopaedic dictionaries published during this period had no entry for 'class', but only for 'class war'.[59] Academics did not really question the issue of whether classes could be said to exist. In the tradition of European political sociology, this presupposition was taken for granted. However, none of the main sociological theorists was a Marxist and each, in his different way, sought to deny the idea of the ultimate polarisation of society between capital and labour.

A common theme was that social divisions were becoming less, rather than more, sharply defined. For example, the Agrarian (later Communist) sociologist, Karel Galla wrote:

In modern times there is a certain standardisation in clothing, food, entertainment and reading matter . . . just as a certain norm of elementary education is being established. This normalisation has removed some of the external differences which used to be so striking.[60]

Jan Mertl, a leading member of the Prague School of Sociology, spoke of the 'continuous growth of the middle class', and suggested that rising educational and economic standards for the working class and falling standards for the upper class were leading to a certain equalisation in society.[61] The most thorough exposition of the theory that the social classes were growing closer together was given in Zdeněk Ullrich's study *Social Structure Today*, written in 1934 at the height of the Depression. The previous year over 1 million people had been unemployed, of whom less than one-third received unemployment benefit. None the less, Ullrich used arguments reminiscent of Weber and Geiger to highlight the growth of the tertiary sector, an increase in the total numbers of employees as opposed to self-employed persons and the impact of political equality for all to suggest 'a continual *rapprochement* . . . between the various strata of the population'.[62] Ullrich was immediately accused of political motivation in his 'shifting of attention . . . from the facts of social differentiation', a claim which he vigorously denied.[63] It remains true that the idea of social divisions being levelled out under the Republic was a popular Establishment idea.

Although there was no attempt at a thorough sociological analysis of Czech inter-war society, certain specific social groups were frequently singled out for examination. There was, for example, considerable interest in the industrial working class, to some extent explained by academics' preoccupation with radical politics. Sociologists were careful to stress that workers did not form a monolithic social group. The existence of both an 'aristocracy of labour' which could potentially be subject to *embourgeoisement*, and of a kind of under-class, a *lumpenproletariat*, was widely accepted, although the exact boundaries of these categories were the cause of some dispute. In general, the former were identified with foremen, or those with special skills, whose standard of living was comparatively high, and who, it was claimed, tended to lose interest in revolutionary politics. The latter comprised 'tramps, beggars, prostitutes, unskilled and seasonal workers', who were feared as being capable, at times of revolutionary turmoil, of the most brutish force, of pillaging and massacres.[64] These divisions had their parallels in both bureaucratic attitudes and in the party ideologies. The notion of there being an underclass of undeserving poor was present in social legislation, although the principle was never openly admitted. Social legislation also recognised foremen as being distinct from the rest of manual workers, whilst communist doctrine, too, spoke of a 'foreign body in the working class'.[65]

Despite the divisions which sociologists claimed to perceive within the working class, they did advance the thesis that there was a working-class psychological and physiological type. It was suggested that the appalling social conditions suffered by the proletariat in the nineteenth century had given rise to a stratum which was often both physically and mentally inferior.[66] However, this gloomy picture of the working class was mitigated by a belief that its economic and social situation was gradually improving. The growing power of trades unions and working-class political parties and social legislation such as the eight-hour day were said to have transformed the quality of working-class life. Improvements in living conditions, dress, standards of education and a greater orientation towards home and family were all detected.[67] Fundamental to such claims was, of course, the desire to depict the worker as a fully integrated member of the community, who no longer subscribed to the doctrines of class war. 'No longer the pariah of national society, [the worker is] an equal amongst equals . . . conscious of his meaning for, and duty towards, the whole nation.'[68]

Rural studies were a major preoccupation of inter-war sociologists. To some extent this was a reflection of the great influence of the Agrarian Party, which helped to sponsor research, and counted many academics amongst its members. Agrarian ideology stressed the idea that 'the village is one family', and some sociologists were fulsome in their descriptions of the harmony of rural life. However, even the most enthusiastic proponents of village unity often testified unwittingly to the existence of a hierarchy based on land-ownership. The Agrarian novelist, Josef Holeček, in his treatise *The Peasantry*, set out the full colloquial hierarchy of rank, although his intention was to stress that differences in economic standing were unimportant in comparison to the bond of belonging to the agricultural community:

The dwarf holder [*domkář*], the small-holder [*chalupník*], the small peasant farmer [*malý sedlák*], the large peasant farmer [*velký sedlák*], the estate owner [*statkář*] and the residual estate owner [*zbytkář*], all are farmers and the peasantry must unite them.[68]

It is clear, moreover, that such social differentiation according to the amount of land held was a crucial factor in the choice of marriage partners, and that 'the peasant farmer marries the peasant farmer's daughter, the small-holder a girl from a small-holding'.[70]

Discussions about the nature of social relationships in the village invariably touched on the quality of the ties between master and man. The fact that the farmer and his labourer often ate at the same table was cited as an example of the closeness of the agricultural community, fostered by mutual service on the land. However, some writers felt that the old patriarchal 'family relationship' was under attack. Josef Holeček, for instance, claimed with some disapproval that, in the independent Republic, the labourer would probably turn for advice to 'the nearest party official [or] . . . the socialist advocate in Prague'.[71] Since 1918, of course, the agricultural labourer had been freed from the constrictions of a semi-feudal work contract and given certain rights to social insurance, and this certainly militated against the old deferential attitudes.

Descriptions of the peasants' physical and psychological characteristics showed the same tendency to condescension as those of the worker. The overall picture of peasant temperament which emerges from sociological studies is, on the whole, unattractive, stressing the narrowness and conservatism of the peasants' outlook on life, their egoism and acquisitiveness. Peasant 'estate consciousness' was said to take on unsympathetic forms, with townspeople viewed as 'parasites and . . . exploiters . . . of the life-giving peasant organism'.[72] However, as in similar studies of the worker, there were attempts to show that the worst features of the peasant character and of rural life were being alleviated by socio-economic and technological changes.[73]

The third social group which came under consideration from sociologists was the intelligentsia. In common with many other nations in continental Europe, there was a distinct sense amongst the Czechs that people with a certain level of education had a cultural unity which, in some way, marked them off from the rest of the population. Although sociologists might suggest that certain intellectual and moral attributes were to be found in 'all income brackets and all types of work', even they tended to use the term 'intelligentsia' colloquially, to refer to those people 'who earn their living by virtue of their school diploma'.[74] Most discussions of the intellectual's psyche and way of life implied that 'the intelligentsia' could be equated with certain kinds of non-manual occupations which usually required a formal education to the level of the *maturita* (secondary school-leaving examination), in other words, with the census category 'officials'.

It is, therefore, hardly surprising that one of the characteristics of the intelligentsia was said to be faith in the sovereignty of education. Many intellectuals seem to have found it difficult to come to terms with a society in which education was no longer a narrow preserve and the growth of mass politics meant that power often lay in the hands of the non-educated. Articles on the 'crisis of the intelligentsia' abound—some of them metaphysical, and others attempting to redefine the political role of the intelligentsia, who could no longer, as in the mid-nineteenth century, expect to lead the nation as of right.[75]

Descriptions of the intelligentsia emphasised the importance to them of social prestige, that good old feeling of being a gentleman. They were said to be very conscious of their 'better' education and their 'better' work, to say nothing of their 'better' housing, their 'better' clothes and their 'better' manners. This sense of superiority is conveyed unwittingly in one sociologist's claim that although books, flowers, pictures and musical instruments might be found in the homes of workers and peasants, 'this is probably the result of copying the decor of the intelligentsia, rather than arising from their own spiritual needs'.[76]

Perhaps the most significant factor emerging from the examination of sociologists' perceptions of class is the importance of the divide between the educated ('the intelligentsia') and the non-educated ('the common people'). The latter were subject to intense scrutiny, partly because of their new political power in an age of mass politics and universal suffrage. Workers were said to be a divided social group, including a lower stratum of the feckless and undeserving, who were associated with disorder. The peasantry, too, were pictured as an internally divided group, but it was stressed that their sense of belonging to a rural community was, none the less, strong. Although the division between town and country may have been weakening under the impact of modernisation, sociologists such as Bláha were still troubled by it. Business and finance were ignored completely, an omission which only serves to strengthen the impression that the intelligentsia (and not least those of their number whose writing are analysed here) had yet to come to terms with the realities of a modern industrial and democratic state.

The most fascinating material for any historical study of this kind is often the unwitting testimony of private individuals, whose informal perceptions of their world sometimes reveal far more than self-conscious sociological analysis, or political polemics about the nature of 'class'. The fourth category of sources to be examined is diverse and somewhat fragmentary: memoirs, reports of the testimony of private individuals in sociological surveys, newspaper articles and letters and archive material. It provides an impressionistic record of inter-war Czech society, to offset and complement the social models offered by bureaucrats, politicians and sociologists. About its authenticity no more can be said than that the examples chosen seem to typify widely-held views.

The stratification model which was most commonly used in colloquial speech by the Czechs acknowledged two main social categories, *páni*, gentlemen, and *lid*, common people. The similarity between this dichotomous division of society and the social differentiation between 'the intelligentsia' and 'the people', so common in academic writings, is obvious. Indeed, a secondary education and the possession of a non-manual job were crucial indicators of whether someone belonged to 'the people' or was, in fact, a 'gentleman', as a survey undertaken in Moravia in the late 1930s revealed. Life-style and social behaviour were also important, and the same survey noted the great social disapprobation felt towards a socially aspiring man who 'blows his nose into his hand'. Family background was another factor used by its respondents in placing someone socially. The survey's conclusion suggested that social mobility in the inter-war Czech Lands was less easy than is sometimes claimed:

It is difficult for a person from a poor background to rise into the 'higher strata', and if he does get there [either because he has founded an independent business or has earned a certain wealth] he is often persistently placed amongst 'the people' simply because of his origins.[77]

It is clear from the evidence available that the four occupational groupings which emerged from the analysis of party programmes—agriculturalists, small businessmen, officials and workers—were also recognised colloquially as social stereotypes. The peasantry, for instance, were willing to express a sense of corporate identity and professional pride in no uncertain terms. A survey in the newspaper *Lidové noviny* in 1924, which asked readers to explain 'Why I like my job', elicited such responses from farmers as 'our profession is the first, the oldest and the most fundamental' and 'We peasants do not learn our trade, we are born to it'. Family traditions seem to have played an important role in these peasants' self-image, as did their strong sense of relationship with the land. One respondent explained:

I am an agriculturalist [*zemědělec*]. Why do I like my job? Because my forebears worked on our soil for more than three hundred years, and cultivated the land which I cultivate today, working from morning to night in the eternal struggle with nature and the gravelly land, just as I struggle today.[76]

There can be no doubt that the agricultural population regarded itself, and was regarded by the rest of society, as a distinct community. It would seem, moreover, that the division between town and country sometimes cut across the class lines envisaged in socialist ideology. Pride in occupation often contrasted with a strong feeling of financial and social disadvantage. The peasants of the East Bohemian village of Dolní Roveň, for instance, told a sociologist who was chronicling village life that: 'Townspeople look down their noses at us, they think that they are "gentlemen", they underestimate us . . . they do not value our work . . . they make fun of us . . . they are stuck up.' Indeed, one agricultural labourer even ventured the opinion that people in towns 'go for walks and amuse themselves. They don't work much, they live in affluence and luxury', and some peasants were reported as describing townspeople as 'drones'.[79]

Scorn was, in fact, only one aspect of the complex attitudes of the rest of society to the peasantry. Journalists on the liberal socio-political journal *Přítomnost* might allow a certain exasperated disdain to show through in their reporting, making claims such as 'The peasantry's immediate concerns end at the village backyard' and 'Peasants rarely indulge in universal ideas'.[80] However, one could equally cite the many Czechs in high places who were proud to boast of their peasant origins, like the rural novelist Josef Knap, who described the peasantry as 'the strongest, healthiest and most positive stratum in the nation'.[81] Overall the impression given is of ambivalence, both in the peasants' perceptions of their own place in society and in the reactions of the rest of society to the peasantry.

Informal evidence about small entrepreneurs is somewhat sparse. It is clear, however, that they were readily identified as a middle group in society. Thus, for example, the 'lonely hearts' page of the women's journal *List paní a dívek* revealed such notices as: 'I would like to introduce my relative, aged 24, to a man of true character. . . . She is a very modest girl, from the middle social strata, and understands both housekeeping and trade'.[82] For a manual worker to become a tradesman of some kind was normally seen as a social advance. One of the respondents to the *Lidové noviny* survey 'Why I like my job' described the progress of his career from factory worker to skilled artisan as 'betterment—from a worker I had become a craftsman, something of an artist'.[83] However, the social position of small businessmen was not necessarily secure. Lack of secondary education and a close association with manual work both carried a certain social stigma. The shoe magnate, Tomáš Baťa, recalling his youth in the 1890s, explained:

When I became apprenticed to my father after primary school, it was clear for me that society was divided into two kinds. Into gentlemen and non-gentlemen . . . Those who went on to study at secondary school were young gentlemen, whilst those who became apprentices were condemned to be non-gentlemen for ever.[84]

Forty years later a survey undertaken in a small Moravian town to investigate links between occupation and social prestige revealed surprisingly similar attitudes.[85] Yet whilst not always honouring small businessmen in practice, the Czechs often recalled with pride that men in high positions were the sons or grandsons of artisans.

The social importance of the division between manual and non-manual labour is very clearly mirrored in informal evidence. For testimony to white-collar employees' sense of social superiority one needs only to consider their hostile reaction to government proposals that workers should be granted old-age and invalidity pensions as part of a unified scheme of social insurance. The following petition sent by six professional organisations to the Ministry of Social Welfare in

1921 illustrates considerable opposition to any blurring of the official distinction made between the two kinds of labour:

> . . . it is materially impossible, and socially highly unjust, to amalgamate the insurance of manual workers . . . under the same conditions as the social insurance of mental workers. . . . [The latter have a] creative mission in the economic and cultural life of the state and of human society. Even allowing for the utmost democracy, the members of our estate have different living conditions to workers . . . [86]

Moreover, clarification of the position of lower-ranking non-manual workers (zřízenci) as employees 'in higher service', eligible for superior social insurance in the terms of the Pensions Acts of 1920 and 1929, gave an institutionalised basis to their sense of distinctiveness. During preparations for the 1930 census, various of their organisations successfully petitioned the State Office of Statistics for them to be granted a separate census category, in acknowledgement of the fact that they were different from manual workers.[87]

Within the ranks of salaried employees, however, there were many internal divisions. The main non-political trade union organisation for officials and zřízenci, the Coborové ústředí, frequently voiced the complaint that:

> It is well known just how complicated divisions amongst officials are. . . . We have separate groups . . . according to whether we are in the public or the private sector. . . . We have further groups according to our level of education. . . . There are far too many groups![88]

The universal use of titles of professional standing such as 'Mr. Engineer' or 'Mr. Draughtsman' is indicative of the intimate connection between someone's job and his social position. An article in the left-wing journal Levá Fronta, in 1932, reported that officials at the Živnostenská banka had just petitioned the management to allow those of their number who had reached the seventeenth wage grade to use the title 'chief official'. Apparently this would 'facilitate their social life'.[89] Such rank-consciousness might be expected to weaken the sense of belonging to a class or 'estate'. Moreover, there was a definite sense of social distinction between officials and zřízenci. The former were readily identified as páni—gentlemen—in the ubiquitous colloquial classification scheme.

The latter, worse paid and almost certainly lacking a grammar school education, were more likely to be regarded as members of the 'common people'.

The term *dělník* (worker) was used by all sectors of society to conjure up a social stereotype. However, workers did not necessarily show an explicit awareness of belonging to a working class as such. Indeed, mention of 'class' tended to be limited to the politically active. Others might express their consciousness of their place in society in terms of 'gentlemen' and 'people', like the wife of a skilled worker in Moravia who knew that 'gentlemen don't eat the left-overs from lunch at dinner-time'; whilst for some, economic hardship was the focal point of their identity.[90] It is clear that some revolutionary sentiment was present, especially amongst the desperate. The communists seem to have been correct in their assessment that the most fertile field for recruitment was amongst the unskilled and the unemployed.[91] Members of the Brno unemployed, questioned at the height of the Depression in 1933, blamed their plight on 'capitalist anarchy in production' and the 'private ownership capitalist order'.[92] However, workers, especially skilled workers, were just as likely to articulate the kind of sentiments of self-respect, pride in work well done and quiet nationalism which promoted political and social stability.

Within the ranks of labour it is clear that there were many distinctions. Social and employment legislation had marked out miners for special treatment, and they do seem to have had a particularly strong sense of separate identity, based on historic guild traditions. A letter to *Lidové noviny* explained:

I work in the Příbram mines, where employment is passed on from father to son. . . . I feel a great sense of estate pride in avowing my membership of that great army of black people. . . who sacrifice their lives for their daily bread and for the good of society . . .[93]

On the other hand, certain categories of workers seem to have felt themselves to be particularly underprivileged. Agricultural workers in Dolní Roveň, for instance, complained that their industrial counterparts had 'big incomes' and 'live better than us'; whilst a servant wrote to *Lidové noviny*: 'I consider housework to be the healthiest and most suitable employment for a girl. . . . But why is it not possible for our employers to treat us a bit more like human beings?'[94] It is, moreover, obvious that some people who were, for whatever reason, unemployed, and certain unskilled and casual workers, had a level of social and economic culture far below that of the rest of the working class. A social worker, writing of her clients for the liberal journal *Přítomnost*, described scenes of great destitution and degradation in the working-class suburbs of Prague:

A small cellar room with only one window, a seven member family. The father has only one leg, he lost the other at the factory. The mother is consumptive. A month ago her third child died of T.B. Now her son is dying. The family lives from what the children get from begging.[95]

Informal sources are revealing not only of conditions at the lowest levels of Czech society; they also help to provide a picture of that society's upper reaches. Contemporary observers were, in fact, often unconvinced that their country possessed a social élite worthy of the name. The Habsburg Court provided memories of 'true' Society—a world in which Countess Sophie Chotková was deemed unworthy to marry the Archduke Franz Ferdinand because she did not belong to one of the twenty families of *ebenbürtig*, and only fabulously wealthy businessmen and financiers, like the Rothschilds, managed to penetrate the inner circle.[96] The Czechs lacked a native aristocracy, apart from the few families who traditionally identified with the national cause, and they had no business dynasty whose capital could rival that of the great Viennese bankers. Yet it is clear that the politicians, bureaucrats, landowners, army officers and people active in the arts who gained entries in the biographical dictionaries of the inter-war period could hardly be called 'little men'. Indeed, the form filled in by those people whose personal details featured in the *Cultural Directory of the Czechoslovak Republic* included an enquiry about whether they came from a 'notable family'— a sure sign of dynasties in the making.[97]

Certain sectors of Czech society were undoubtedly marked out by their wealth and affluent life-style. Hunting and riding were regularly cited as pastimes by businessmen in the various Who's Whos, and some, like the textile barons, the Bartoň-Dobeníns, were revealed to collect works of art, and even to own castles.[98] However, wealth was far from being an absolute criterion of social rank. Many leading figures in society lived quite modestly, and intellectuals, in particular, were not noted for their affluence. Membership of a club was perhaps a better indicator of whether someone belonged to the highest circles of society. Writer and journalist Jaromír John explained of Prague:

The stratum which forms Society in the highest form here [as exemplified by] Společenský klub na Příkopě and Společenský klub na Střeleckém ostrově is comprised of intellectuals—officials, professors, journalists, officers, doctors, advocates, writers, and a small number from the agricultural, entrepreneurial, trade and banking strata, who tend to be represented in the third Prague club, the Autoklub.[99]

The most exclusive social formations of all were often of a less formal kind—notably the Friday afternoon meetings of intellectuals at the home of the writer Karel Čapek. Masaryk and Beneš were frequent guests, along with leading academics, journalists, writers and professional men. One of the founder members noted that, as the reputation of the meetings grew, people felt that participation would help to further their ambitions, and fathers took their sons along, 'as if they were bestowing them with a dowry'.[100]

The overall impression of Czech 'Society' does not suggest a uniform and homogeneous social group. Intellectual observers, for example, were somewhat scornful of the claimed vulgarity of the *nouveaux riches*. The anonymous author of an article entitled 'Notes from Prague Society' (published in 1924) spoke with disdain of the Czechs' 'upper ten thousand',

in number 100–150 individuals. They have enough money, they have adapted themselves to the way of life . . . Amongst the Czechs it is sufficient that a smoked meat shop should have become a big business twenty years ago, and that the family members are fashionably dressed.[101]

Perhaps one can detect a note of sourness because the economic bourgeoisie were taking over a social role which the intelligentsia had previously considered as its own. It is clear that many Czechs had risen up the social scale very quickly after 1918 and initially there was a tendency to eschew the conventions of polite society as being a relic of the Habsburg past. The writer Edward Valenta explained that this 'pettiness' expressed itself in the 'wearing of tan shoes with an evening dress' and 'smacking one's lips whilst at table'.[102] Twenty years of independence was hardly long enough for the nascent upper strata of Czech society to take on a great appearance of homogeneity and to develop their own distinct social ethos.

The Czechs of the inter-war period do not, on the whole, seem to have had a very clear sense of 'class'; they tended to locate themselves in the social hierarchy in terms of education, or specific occupation, or perhaps the somewhat nebulous quality of being a 'gentleman'. None the less, the labels and divisions presented by government agencies, political parties and sociologists do seem to have impinged on popular perceptions of society. In particular, the distinctions recognised in social legislation, once institutionalised, were readily accepted as natural and fitting, especially by those whom they benefited. The picture presented overall is of a fragmented upper stratum, or strata, four basic occupational groupings, and a group of unfortunates whom social insurance provisions had failed to rescue from a life of considerable degradation.

Finally a brief discussion of the social imagery in the Czech novel of the inter-war period will conclude this analysis of 'subjective' evidence. Contemporary critics often deplored the narrow range of social themes in Czech literature, which they castigated as 'petty bourgeois' and 'provincial' in spirit. Paul (Pavel) Eisner, as a German one of the more dispassionate observers of the Czech literary scene, blamed this on 'Czech life, with its lack of social stratification and its insubstantial social traditions'. He was, however, forced to conclude that although Czech society in the independent Republic was rapidly becoming more variegated, its writers had yet to take full account of the new social reality.[103]

A noticeable feature of the inter-war novel is its almost total failure to depict the upper reaches of society—a characteristic shared by most of the categories of source material discussed above. The two best-known novels of Prague patrician society, Čapek-Chod's *Turbina* and Tilschová's *An Old Family* were both published in 1916, and there was no equivalent from the independent Republic.[104] In so far as businessmen did feature in the inter-war novel, they were depicted as caricatures and often, significantly, given names which were more recognisably German or Jewish than Czech. G.H. Bondy in Karel Čapek's *Factory for the Absolute*, for example, is a somewhat comic figure and totally obsessed with the profit motive.[105] Pressinger, the factory owner in Benjamin Klička's *Brody*, is an evil exploiter of the masses who exercises the twentieth-century equivalent of *droit de seigneur* to fill the whole neighbourhood with illegitimate children.[106] Convincing portrayals of high intellectual circles are almost as rare; the main exceptions are the novels of Marie Pujmanová, herself from an old-established medical family. Unlike most other novelists, she knew this society from the inside, and understood its social indicators.[107] The typical Czech author, however, came from a more modest background than Pujmanová, and according to Paul Eisner, 'Even his university professor is unconvincing. His bank director is impossible, and if he ventures, on paper of course, into the milieu of the aristocracy, we feel sorry for him.'[108]

The typical hero of the Czech novel from this period was a 'little man'. Indeed, Karel Čapek even wrote a novel entitled *An Ordinary Life*, in which he chronicled the hidden dramas in the life of a railway official.[109] Čapek's writings tend to eulogise the ordinary man, great in nothing but his humanity, and they proved enormously popular. The last novel to be published in his life-time. *The First Rescue Party*, was an instant bestseller and in many ways epitomises the Masarykian intellectual's view of Czech society. Its theme was a common one—the story of a rescue party in a mining disaster. Ordinary miners, a pit deputy and a mining engineer work side by side in a vain attempt to rescue the trapped men. Courage and quiet heroism are shown as characteristics found in all social strata, and at a time of crisis social differences are put aside in a show of manly solidarity. Even the pit's managers show some humanity—after the disaster they send the crippled hero Standa Půlpán (the surname means 'half gentleman') to complete the secondary education which he had been forced to abandon on the death of his aunt several years previously.[110] The communist critic, Julius Fučík, wrote that he had read the book with some workers who had praised it except for this final point, which they found too much to take.[111]

Although Bohemia and Moravia were leading industrial regions, remarkably few of the Czech novels published in the inter-war period depicted the life of the industrial proletariat. A survey undertaken in 1937 claimed that of over 4000 novels analysed, only 49 dealt with either workers or the industrial milieu.[112] Novels of the working class were often somewhat tendentious and unconvincing. Descriptions of the minutiae of everyday working-class life and plausible dialogue were rare, probably because most authors had no more knowledge of this environment that they had of the highest social circles. In the author's mind, the didactic purpose of his novel was often more important anyway than the need for authenticity. This is certainly true of Olbracht's *Anna the Proletarian*, in which a naive country-born serving-maid develops into a class-conscious proletarian. The novel ends with a set-piece of social confrontation in which Anna meets her former employer by chance during the unrest of December 1920.

In front of her in the cold and damp atmosphere of that December day stood the evil face of the class enemy . . . It is for these champagne-coloured shoes and silk stockings that there will be murder today. It is indeed for the charming hat . . . and the flower made of bright-coloured silk that workers' blood flowed yesterday . . . Anna the flaxen haired serving maid stood up tall . . . 'You would shoot at us? Well, we will shoot at you, too, Madam'. Her eyes blazed, she turned and left.[113]

A Marxist sympathiser, Fedor Soldan, writing in 1933, suggested that the traditions of Czech literature encouraged writers to depict an 'undifferentiated national whole'— nineteenth-century nationalism had needed to encourage supra-class unity, and twentieth-century authors still followed this model.[114] It is true that far more graphic descriptions of social divisions and problems can be found in newspaper *feuilletons* than in novels. The overall impression is that literary creations failed, for a variety of reasons, to keep fully abreast with social change and to create a convincing picture of a multifaceted industrial society.

The Realities of Class

A wide range of sources have been analysed above in order to illustrate contemporary perceptions of the social order in the Czech Lands between the two World Wars. Although the term 'class' was rarely used, except in a political context, it is clear from the evidence that Czechs were conscious of a variety of social hierarchies and distinctions, be they the broad societal divisions between 'gentlemen' and 'people', or the more narrowly specific occupational groupings of salaried employees, small businessmen, peasants and manual workers. It remains to examine some of the demonstrable realities of social and economic inequality in the Czech Lands during this period, and to integrate these with the images already discussed.

Contemporaries often played down the importance of income as a socially divisive factor. The impoverished official was a common social stereotype, found in the political party programmes and newspaper articles alike. There were many observations too about the lack of a substantive upper class of wealth.[115] Yet there can be no doubt that material inequalities in the Czech Lands were considerable. The State Office of Statistics produced periodic analyses of family budgets which make it possible to trace an intimate connection between income and occupation. The report on 'Consumption in the families of manual workers, lower-ranking non-manual workers and officials' from 1931–32, for instance, gives a clear indication of income differentials. The average annual income of the head of the household for those families participating in this survey ranged from 7066 crowns* for unskilled workers; 10,919 crowns for skilled workers; 16,132 crowns for foremen and master-craftsmen; 15,551 crowns for zřízenci; 21,923 crowns for lower-grade state officials; 22,136 crowns for lower-grade officials in the private sector; 32,512 crowns for higher-grade officials in the private sector to 37,871 crowns for higher-grade officials in state service. Patterns of consumption reflected these income differentials.[116]

---

*There were approximately 140 crowns to the pound.

The most detailed treatment of higher income levels can be found in an analysis based on the tax statistics from 1928. In that year 13,566 people in Bohemia and Moravia earned more than 100,000 crowns a year; 308 people had an annual income of more than 1 million crowns, and 24 received more than 5 million crowns a year. Indeed, the average income of this latter group was actually just over 11 million crowns, at a time when 50 per cent of wage earners received less than 6000 crowns a year. Salaries formed only a small proportion of total annual revenue for the very wealthy. As in other industrial countries, the upper stratum of wealth in the inter-war Czech Lands supported itself mainly from business profits and investment income. Landed wealth continued to be an important source of income, despite the land reforms; it came second only to business profits for those in receipt of more than 1 million crowns a year.[117] The impersonal nature of the tax statistics make it impossible to tell how many of the very wealthy were actually Czech, rather than German or Jewish. However, there can be no doubt that some Czechs were included in the highest income bracket. Tomáš Baťa, for example, was a self-confessed multi-millionaire.

Certain sectors of the community had particularly low standards of living. Agricultural labourers were notoriously badly paid, which often led to resentment of the urban proletariat; figures for 1930 suggest that their average wages were only 51 per cent of the average for all manual employees.[118] Moreover, the old, the sick and the unemployed frequently faced great economic hardship. The minimum guaranteed pension for a worker was only 500 crowns a year, whilst unemployed persons who were not eligible for benefits under the Ghent system received only 10 crowns a week, if single, and 20 crowns, if married.[119] These subsidies were not payable to house owners, even if they were otherwise totally destitute, neither, until 1935, were they payable to people who had been self-employed.[120] The levels of material deprivation suffered by the lowest income groups indeed make it possible to describe them as an 'underclass'.

Just as the average income in the inter-war Czech Lands was low by the standards of Western Europe and the USA, so the average size of dwellings was, for the majority of the population, smaller than in comparable industrialised countries. None the less, both the size and quality of housing remained one of the most fundamental indicators of social divisions, as, in urban districts, did geographical location. The two urban housing censuses of 1921 and 1930 make it possible to compare the housing standards of the major social groups. It is clear, for instance, that the working class were far more likely to live in one room, or one room and a kitchen, than either non-manual employees or the self-employed. Similarly, workers were far less likely to have bathrooms, inside lavatories, running water, gas or electricity in their homes than other groups. Officials' dwellings were by far the most spacious and well-equipped. But the qualitative difference in housing conditions between manual workers and *zřízenci* is also striking.[121]

As in other countries, certain residential areas in the major Czech towns were associated with particular income groups. In Prague, for example, the highest rents and the largest flats were to be found in Josefov in the Old Town; in 1930 only 6.7 per cent of the inhabitants of this district were manual workers. Dejvice, Bubeneč and Vinohrady all contained large and expensive family houses; the Čapek brothers shared a villa in the latter suburb. At the other end of the social scale, Žižkov, Vysočany and Košíře were characterised by high-density and often sub-standard working-class housing.[122] According to two surveys undertaken in the late 1920s and early 1930s, over 10 per cent of the inhabitants of Vysočany and Košíře fell into the category of 'socially needy'.[123] Moreover, the acute housing shortage, and often high rents, led workers to construct 'emergency colonies', often little better than shanty towns, of which the worst examples were Na Krejcáru and Na Židovských Pecích in Žižkov. The living conditions for those at the bottom of the social scale sometimes scarcely merited description as 'housing'.[124]

It is clear that styles of life in the inter-war Czech Lands were closely allied to income and occupation. Educational opportunity, or the lack of it, was often a crucial factor in determining the life chances of the various social groups. Careers in state service, for example, depended very rigidly on formal educational qualifications. The *maturita* (secondary-school leaving certificate) was a prerequisite for executive posts in the Civil Service, and for admission to the officers' training academy. It also bestowed an automatic right to a place in a university. In this 'paradise for the Ph.D.' academic achievement was often a stepping-stone to success in business and finance too, as well as in government.[125]

Although education at all levels was open to the talented children of the lower strata, both financial constraints and the rigidity of the system were often a barrier to their successful completion of a secondary or higher education. The majority of children, in fact, never got beyond the elementary school, and a survey of secondary school graduates in the Czech Lands in the academic year 1933–34 came to the general conclusion that:

> For a worker to put his son, or indeed his daughter, through a complete secondary education entails a great sacrifice. It requires not only a considerable financial sacrifice, but also great courage, and an important re-orientation of the mentality of a manual wage-earner . . . to take this step.[126]

Although there were some notable examples of 'poor boys made good', amongst them the first President of the Republic, Tomáš Masaryk, the son of a coachman, children from professional families were far more likely to achieve academic success than those from the poorer strata. In 1933/34 there were 128 secondary school graduates for every 10,000 officials in the Czech Lands, 25 for every 10,000 *zřízenci*, 13 for every 10,000 self-employed persons, and only 4 for every 10,000 manual workers.[127]

In a society where industrialisation had proceeded slowly, and where there was little or no native aristocracy, it is hardly surprising that education was of such importance as a means to social mobility. However, in the inter-war years, burgeoning family connections can be traced in the higher reaches of society. There are many instances of second generation business entrepreneurs, amongst them the Havel brothers, co-owners of the Lucerna palace in Prague, and both actively involved in the film industry, or Joe [sic] Hartman, a leading figure in the sugar industry, who was the son of a director of the Schoelle sugar works, and went on to marry a daughter of the banker, Jaroslav Preiss. In politics, too, family connections were not unimportant. Of President Masaryk's four children,

Herbert died during the war, and Olga married abroad, but Jan was Ambassador to London, and became Foreign Secretary after the Second World War, whilst Alice was a Deputy in the Revolutionary National Assembly, and afterwards President of the Czechoslovak Red Cross. It would, however, be an exaggeration to speak of a distinct upper class, in which family connections had an overriding influence on access to power and authority.[128]

None the less, all the evidence suggests that certain groups in Czech society did wield a disproportionate influence in comparison to their numbers, which is as might be expected. Most members of the business and financial élite played little active role in party politics at the parliamentary level, although a number of them were members of the National Democratic Party.[129] However, it is easy to demonstrate a close relationship between business and government in the inter-war period. Jaroslav Preiss, for example, was one of the architects of financial policy in the early years of the Republic. Moreover, many politicians had business interests. During the third electoral period of 1929/35, 115 deputies held 345 places on the boards of a variety of industrial, commercial and financial enterprises.[130] Ministers had to renounce their directorships when actually in office. However, concerns such as the Škoda armament works, which was dependent on government orders, got around this restriction by informing ministers that a place on the board would be theirs as soon as their term of office came to an end.[131] It was a very good way to involve public figures in reciprocal services.

Agrarian capital also had considerable political influence. The Agrarian Party was able to bring about the reintroduction of tariffs on grain products in 1925 and 1926, despite the fact that this hit trade with the other countries of the Little Entente, and also aroused the bitter opposition of the socialist parties.[132] Moreover, although the interests of agriculture and industry were sometimes at odds, it should not be forgotten that the Agrární banka had considerable industrial investments, and that many industrialists were also landowners.

In comparison, the ordinary citizen, the far from wealthy 'little Czech man', had scant influence over the running of his country. Although there was universal suffrage, the system of proportional representation, which involved voting for a party list rather than for a specific candidate, meant that representatives had little sense of direct responsibility to their constituencies. The party reigned supreme; the average Parliamentary Deputy or Senator was unable to exercise much personal initiative, and real power was largely the monopoly of a few party leaders, who might, of course, have risen from the lower social strata.[133]

Both manual workers and salaried employees were very highly unionised, especially in the period immediately following independence. However, the trades union movement remained highly fragmented, as it had done under the Habsburgs, and its initial strength in the uncertain times following the war proved a transitory phenomenon. Organised protest had its occasional successes: the miners' strikes of 1921 and 1922, for example, were in part instrumental in securing them superior social benefits.[134] None the less, the ordinary citizen had little control over his economic and political destiny, although society was sufficiently open to allow some talented individuals to rise through the system.

Conclusion

Perhaps the strongest impression to be gained of inter-war Czech society is of a people who identified strongly with the image of the 'little man'. This image was particularly well expressed by the Agrarian politician, Antonín Švehla: 'The great majority of our nation is made up of little poor people, small and medium peasant farmers and industrial workers . . . small tradesmen, artisans and shopkeepers, officials and members of the liberal professions.'[135] The definition is, of course, platitudinous—in any industrial society one would expect wealthy businessmen and landowners to be in a minority. Moreover, as has been suggested above, inter-war Czechoslovakia had no outstanding claim to be considered a state run by ordinary citizens. Yet the notion of the Czechs as 'little men' has been propagated by both contemporaries and historians alike as a unique and essential truth about the nature of inter-war society.[136] There was a certain element of political rhetoric in the appeal to the 'little man'. Political leaders, especially in the early years of the Republic, needed to encourage a sense of identification with the state amongst the peasantry and the industrial working class, both of whom had become much more aware of their potential strength as a result of the war. Masarykian philosophy, with its emphasis on the dignity of labour and the value of each individual to the community, however lowly his occupation, tended to promote political and social stability. Likewise, the concept of the 'little man', a social hero who was not identifiable with any one specific class or occupational group, encouraged harmony in Czechoslovak society.

However, identification with the little man was more than a convenient political device; it also revealed a narrow and somewhat anachronistic conception of national society. Until independence, the Czechs had been dominated both economically and politically by Vienna. The period between the wars was one of state building, during which new economic and political élites came to the fore. Few Czech families had been prominent for more than one or two generations, and twenty years of independence was too short a period for the emerging national élites to develop fully the ethos of an upper class, or to establish themselves as such in social perceptions.

The highest placed social group to be readily identified by contemporaries was 'officials'—not, of course, the private secretaries to government ministers, but rather badly paid minor civil servants and grammar-school teachers. Their social position was assured; they had normally been educated at least to the level of the *maturita*, and they were identified colloquially as 'gentlemen'. Beneath them came *zřízenci*, lower-ranking non-manual workers, a social group which had increased in numbers rapidly as a result of economic changes from the 1890s onwards. Their status as 'employees in higher service' was confirmed by the Social Insurance Acts of the 1920s, and the favourable treatment afforded by social and employment legislation provided an institutionalised basis for their sense of separate identity.[137] Their life chances, in terms of income, housing and educational opportunity, were greater than those of manual workers. However, they were still likely to be classed colloquially amongst the 'common people'.

The two traditional groups in society, peasant farmers and small entrepreneurs, were regarded with much sentimental attachment, though it is clear that these occupations were awarded a fairly low social status when compared to jobs which required the completion of a grammar school or a university education. Both of these groups tended to criticise the prestige accorded to formal educational achievements, which their members usually lacked.[138]

Although it was far from homogeneous, the working class was the only social group commonly referred to as a class by contemporaries. Differences in levels of skill, and distinctions between agricultural and industrial labour, may have formed the basis for divisions of interest which cut across the unity of the class. None the less, many manual workers, especially in industry, do seem to have shared a certain common social identity. Social and employment legislation marked them off from white-collar employees, and also largely ignored the distinctions between the skilled, the semi-skilled and the unskilled. There was, however, a loosely-defined 'underclass', composed of casual workers and certain categories of unskilled labour, who did not share fully in the benefits conferred by such legislation. They were regarded by the Communist Party and sociologists alike as potential revolutionaries.

The social groups outlined above were basically occupational categories, which were distinguished by the census and party political programmes, and were readily accepted as social stereotypes. Perhaps the most significant divisions which appear to have influenced social perceptions in the inter-war period were dichotomous—the distinction between town and country, manual and non-manual labour and the educated and the uneducated—and all cut across the more obvious barriers of class. Similarly, rank-consciousness, which was particularly strong amongst white-collar workers, was antithetical to the formation of all-inclusive social classes. The structure of Czech society was still far removed from that of an advanced capitalist country like Great Britain. It is clear that the socio-economic inheritance of the Habsburg past continued to counterbalance the forces of change, even after the Czechs gained their independence in 1918.

Notes

1. B. Markolous, 'Kluby a jejich anglická tradice', in *Magazin dp*, iii (1933), p. 107. (Jaromír John was a pen name.)
2. See, for example, Victor S. Mamatey and Radomir Luža, *A History of the Czechoslovak People, 1918–1948* (Princeton, 1973), pp. 44–45; František Charvát, Jiří Linhart and Jiří Večerník, *Sociálně třídní struktura Československa* (Prague, 1978), passim.
3. Mamatey and Luža, *op. cit.*, pp. 42–3.
4. Heinz O. Ziegler, *Die berufliche und soziale Gliederung der Bevölkerung in der Tschechoslowakei* (Brno, 1936), Übersicht 1, no page reference.
5. Doreen Warriner, 'Czechoslovakia and Central European Tariffs', in *Slavonic Review*, xi (1933), p. 321.
6. See Otto Urban, *Kapitalismus a česká společnost v 19 století* (Prague, 1978), pp. 236–7, 269 for comments from Karel Havliček and Jaroslav Preiss.
7. Ziegler, *op. cit.*, pp. 64, 70 and Übersicht 39.
8. Václav Průcha, 'Složení průmyslového dělnictva v předmnichovském Československu', in *Revue dějin socialismu*, special issue (1966). p. 973.
9. Alois Rozehnal, *Odborové hnutí v Československé republice* (New York, 1953), p. 30.
10. *Ibid.*, 20–8.
11. Bernard Michel, *Banques et banquiers en Autriche au debut du 20ᵉ siècle* (Paris, 1976), pp. 336–7; Norman Stone, 'Army and Society in the Habsburg Monarchy, 1900–1914', *Past and present*, xxxiii (1966), p. 98.
12. Helmut Slapnicka, 'Der neue Staat und die bürokratische Kontinuität; die Entwicklung der Verwaltung, 1918–1938', in Karl Bosl (ed.), *Die demokratischparlamentarische Struktur der ersten Tschechoslowakischen Republik* (Munich, 1975), pp. 123–4.
13. Jozef Faltus, 'Nostrifikácia po 1. svetovej vojne ako doležity nástroj upevnenia českého finančného kapitálu', *Politická ekonomie*, ix (1961), pp. 28–37.
14. Information compiled by the author from Miroslav Buchvalek (ed.), *Dějiny Československa v dátech* (Prague, 1968); *Československo* (Prague, 1936–41); *Kulturní adresář ČSR* (Prague, 1934); František Sekanina (ed.), *Album representantů všech oborů veřejného života československého* (Prague, 1927).
15. Jan Doležal and Zdeněk Ullrich, 'Výzkum abiturientů českých středních škol v zemi České a Moravsko-slezské ve školním roce 1933/34', *Statistický obzor*, xvi (1935), p. 198.
16. *Ibid.*, p. 201.
17. Quoted in Vladimir Dubský, *Odbory v počátcích Československého státu* (Prague, 1978), p. 37.
18. See Margaret Smales, 'Class, Estate and Status, Czechoslovakia 1918–1938', (Ph.D. thesis Open.University, 1983), pp. 32–5.
19. E. Čapek, 'Politický vývoj a strany v československé republice' in *Československá vlastivěda*, vol. 5 (Prague, 1931), pp. 441–3.

20. F. Gregory Campbell, *Confrontation in Central Europe, Weimar Germany and Czechoslovakia* (Chicago, 1975), pp. 217–18.
21. *Ibid.*, p. 259.
22. Karel Čapek, *Na břehu dnů*, 2nd edn. (Prague, 1978), p. 256.
23. *Sbírka zákonů a nařízení státu Československého*, iii (1920), p. 265.
24. Antonín Chyba, *Postavení dělnické třídy v kapitalistickém Československu* (Prague, 1961), p. 51.
25. *Recensement de la population dans la république tchécoslovaque au 15 février 1921*, vol. 2, part 4 (Prague, 1927), p. 84.
26. *Sčítání lidu v republice československé ze dne 1. prosince 1930*, vol. 2, part 1 (Prague, 1935), p. 17.
27. *Ibid*, p. 17.
28. *Recensement, op. cit.*, p. 84.
29. See Chapter 4, pp. 124 below.
30. One of which is quoted below. p. 95.
31. Evžen Štern, 'Deset let naší sociální politiky' in *Sociální revue*, x (1929), p. 17; 'O sociální pojištení dělnické', *Akademie*, xxxi (1929), p. 148.
32. *Československá vlastivěda*, vol. 6 (Prague, 1930), pp. 118–35.
33 SÚA Praha MSP, 2g/Kl 1921–24, 8151. The age at which workers' widows received pensions was reduced to 60 in 1928.
34. *Sbírka zákonů a nařízení*, iii (1920), p. 155.
35 *Sociální revue*, vi (1925), pp. 488–90.
36. *Sociální revue*, vii (1926), p. 193.
37. *Sbírka zákonů a nařízení*, xii (1929), pp. 195–6.
38. See Smales, *op. cit.*, pp. 77–9.
39. See Chapter 2, p. 20.
40. For a background study of the various political parties, see Vladimír Krechler, *Politické strany v předmnichovském Československu* (Prague, 1967).
41. *Program československé národní demokracie* (Prague, 1919), p. 3.
42. *Program a organisační řád 'republikánské strany zemědělského a malorolnického lidu'* (Prague, 1922), p. 9; Dušan Uhlíř, 'Dva směry v československém agrárním hnutí a rozchod Karla Praska s republikánskou stranou', *Sborník historický* xviii (1971), p. 136.
43 *Protokol šestého řádného sjezdu KSČ* (Prague, 1931), p. 117; *Protokol čtvrtého řádného sjezdu komunistické strany Československa* (Prague, 1927), pp. 41–2.
44. *Program československé sociálně-demokratické strany dělnické* (Prague, 1930), pp. 12, 28; *Program a zásady československé strany národně-socialistické* (Prague, 1933), pp. 87–9.
45. *Program . . . národně-socialistické, op. cit.*, p. 89.
46. *Program . . . republikánské, op. cit.*, p. 11.
47. Bedřich Vašek, *Rukojeť křesťánské sociologie* (Olomouc, 1935), p. 148; *Program a organisační řád československé živnostensko-obchodnické strany středostavovské* (Prague, 1929), p. 3; *Program . . . národně-socialistické, op. cit.*, p. 92.
48. *Obnova lidské společnosti* (Prague, 1920), p. 46; *Program . . . živnostensko . . .*, p. 7.

49. *Program . . . živnostensko . . ., op. cit.*, p. 11.
50. *Program československé národní demokracie* (Prague, 1919), p. 44; *Obnova, op. cit.*, p. 46
51. *Program československé strany národně-socialistické přijaty . . . 1918* (Prague, 1928), p. 8; *Program československé sociálně-demokratické strany dělnické* (Brno, 1919), p. 3.
52. *Obnova, op. cit.*, p. 47.
53. *Program . . . živnostensko . . ., op. cit.*, p. 4; *Program . . . republikánské . . ., op. cit.*, p. 63.
54. *Obnova, op. cit.*, p. 39–43; *Program . . . národní demokracie, op. cit.*, pp. 39–41.
55. *Protokol prvního řádneho sjezdu komunistické strany československé* (Prague, n.d.), p. 12; *Program pátého řáného sjezdu komunistické strany Československa* (Prague, n.d.), pp. 9, 207.
56. *Program . . . sociálně . . . 1930, op. cit.*, p. 15.
57. *Obnova, op. cit.*, pp. 15–16.
58. *Program . . . národní demokracie, op. cit.*, p. 42.
59. Emanuel Chalupny (ed.), *Slovník národohospodářský, sociální a politický*, vol. 3 (Prague, 1929), p. 582.
60. Karel Galla, *Třídy ve společnost a třídní boj* (Prague, 1930), p. 25.
61. Jan Mertl, 'K otázce společenských tříd', *Naše Doba*, xxxiv (1926), p. 98.
62. Zdeněk Ullrich, 'Sociální struktura dneška', *Populační, hospodářský, ideový, politický dnešek* (Prague, 1934), p. 43.
63. František Fajfr, 'Nivelisace dnešní společnosti', *Čin*, vi (1934), p. 1011; Zdeněk Ullrich, 'Nivelisace dnešní společnosti', *Sociální problémy*, iv (1935), p. 61.
64. Jan Mertl, 'Dělnictvo jako společenská třída', *Sociální revue*, x (1929), p. 435.
65. See p. 85 above.
66. Mertl, 'Dělnictvo . . .', *op. cit.*, pp. 430–1.
67. Inocenc Arnošt Blaha, *Sociologie sedláka a dělníka*, 2nd edn (Prague, 1937), pp. 72–9.
68. Jaroslav Hanáček, 'K otázce dělníkova sociálního sebevědomí', *Sociologická revue*, xii (1946), pp. 34–5. The research for this article was undertaken just before the outbreak of the Second World War.
69. Josef Holeček, *Selství* (Prague, 1928), p. 381.
70. Karel Galla, *Dolní Roveň* (Prague, 1929), p. 328.
71. Holeček, *op.cit.*, p. 355.
72. Blaha, *Sociologie . . ., op. cit.*, pp. 118, 149.
73. *Ibid.*, pp. 190–1.
74. Emanuel Rádl, *Krise inteligence* (Prague, 1928), p. 7; Inocenc Arnošt Blaha, *Sociologie inteligence* (Prague, 1927), passim.
75. Rádl, *op. cit.*; F.X. Šalda, 'Krise inteligence', *Šaldův zápisník*, iii (1930–31).
76. Blaha, *Sociologie inteligence, op. cit.*, pp. 270–1, 183.
77. Leonard Boček, 'Jsou obchodníci, živnostníci, řemeslníci a nižší

úředníci 'pány' či 'lidem'?', *Sociologická revue*, vol. 11, no. 1/2 (1940), p. 77.
78. Gel, *O lidských povoláních, 555 autorů napsalo* (Prague, 1931), pp. 73, 70, 76.
79. Galla, *Dolní Roveň, op. cit.*, pp. 311, 315.
80. Quoted in Antonín Matula, 'Kulturní politika republikánské strany', *Brazda*, vol. 9, no. 3 (1929), p. 34.
81. 'Proč sympatisuji s agrárním hnutím', *Brázda*, vol, 16, no. 8 (1935), p. 114.
82. *List paní a dívek*, no. 119 (7), 1927, p. 19.
83. Gel, *op. cit.*, pp. 141–2.
84. Quoted in Antonín Cekota, *Geniální podnikatel Tomáš Baťa* (Toronto, 1981), p. 35.
85. Boček, *op. cit.*, pp. 75–6.
86. SÚA Praha MSP D2g/P 1922–29, 673/1921.
87. *Sčítání . . . 1930, op. cit.*, p. 17.
88. *Odborové ústředí 'Československý svaz úřednických a zřízeneckých organisací'* (Prague, 1922), p. 1.
89. *Levá fronta*, vol. 2, no. 4 (1932), p. 7.
90. Hanáček, *op. cit.*, p. 45.
91. See p. 85 above.
92. Bruno Zwicker, 'K sociologii nezaměstnanosti', *Sociologická revue*, vi (1935), p. 41.
93. Gel, *op. cit.*, p. 86.
94. Galla, Dolní Roveň, *op. cit.*, p. 314; Gel, *op. cit.*, p. 9.
95. Marcela Procházková, 'Lid z periferie', *Přítomnost*, vol. 3, no. 5 (1926), p. 73.
96. See Michel, *Banques . . ., op. cit.*, p. 335.
97. *Kulturní adresář ČSR* (Prague, 1934), p. 15.
98. *Ibid.*, passim; *České biografie* (Prague, 1936–41), passim.
99. Markolous, *op. cit.*, p. 108.
100. Ferdinand Peroutka, 'Peroutka o Pátcích', *Proměny*, vol. 18 (1931), p. 51.
101. 'Glossy z pražské společnosti' in *Přítomnost*, i (1924), p. 673.
102. Edvard Valenta, *Žil jsem s miliardářem* (Cologne, 1980), p. 24.
103. Pavel Eisner, 'Český autor žije nesprávně', *Rozpravy Aventinum*, vol. 9, no. 1 (1933–34), p. 3.
103. Karel Matěj Čapek-Chod, *Turbina* (Prague, 1916); Anna Maria Tilschová, *Stará Rodina* (Prague, 1916).
105. Karel Čapek, *Továrna na absolutno* (Prague, 1922).
106. Benjamin Klička, *Brody* (Prague, 1926).
107. See, for example, her *Lidé na křižovatce* (Prague, 1937).
108. Eisner, *op. cit.*, p. 4.
109. Karel Čapek, *Obyčejný život* (Prague, 1934).
110. Karel Čapek, *První parta* (Prague, 1937).
111. Julius Fučík's review from *Rudé právo* is quoted in an editorial comment to the 1954 edition, p. 195.

112. Jaroslav Sima, 'Literatura a společnost', *Dělnická osvěta*, vol. xxv (1939), p. 183.
113. Ivan Olbracht, *Anna proletářka* (Prague, 1961), p. 221. This novel was first published in 1928.
114. Fedor Soldan, 'Bída české prózy', *Rozpravy Aventinum*, vol. 9, no. 3 (1933), p. 29.
115. For example, see Holeček, *Selství*, *op. cit.*, p. 421.
116. *Československá statistika*, vol. 152, series xix (Prague, 1937), p. 6.
117. Hospodárske dejiny Československa (Bratislava, 1974), p. 203–4.
118. Chyba, *Postavení* . . . *op. cit.*, p. 88.
119. Evžen Stern, 'Kritický rozbor péče o nezaměstnané v Československu', *Socialní revue*, xiii (1932), p. 21.
120. Jaromír Nečas, *Nezaměstnanost a podpůrná péče v Československu* (Prague, 1938), passim.
121. Smales, *op. cit.*, pp. 245–6.
122. Charvát, *op. cit.*, p. 38; *Stará dělnická Praha* (Prague, 1981), p. 261.
123. Otakar Machotka, *Socialně-potřebné rodiny v hlavním městě Praze* (Prague, 1936), p. 30; M. Nečasová-Poubová, 'Školní prospěch dítěte a jeho sociální poměry', in *Sociální revue*, x (1929), pp. 33, 35.
124. Vanda Tůmanová, *Pražské nouzové kolonie* (Prague, 1971), passim.
125. Smales, *op. cit.*, pp. 249–53.
126. Doležal, *op. cit.*, p. 201.
127. *Ibid.*, p. 198.
128. Smales, *op. cit.*, pp. 255–8.
129. Amongst them Jaroslav Preiss and Joe Hartmann.
130. Alice Teichová, 'O výdělečných činnostech členů poslanecké sněmovny ve volebním období 1929–1935' in *ČSČH*, i (1955), pp. 112–13.
131. Alice Teichová, *An Economic Background to Munich* (Cambridge, 1974), pp. 205–6.
132. Mamatey and Luža, *op. cit.*, pp. 127, 130, 147.
133. Josef Macek, *Parlament zevnitř* (Prague, 1932), passim.
134. Leonard Bianchi, *Dejiny štátu a práva na uzemí Československa v období kapitalismu*, vol. 2 (Bratislava, 1971), p. 242.
135. Quoted in *Idea československého státu*, vol. 1 (Prague, 1936), p. 232.
136. See Mamatey and Luža, *op. cit.*, pp. 44–5.
137. See p. 80 above.
138. See p. 84 above.

CHAPTER FOUR

Élites, Estate and Strata: Class in West Germany since 1945

Angi Rutter

The Historical Context

When asked to describe the shape of society in the Federal Republic, the chances are that the average West German might, whilst denying the existence of a class society, none the less proceed to talk of his or her fellow countrymen using a terminological instrumentarium which, although often a rather diffuse combination of elements such as 'estate', 'stratum' or 'élite', is as equally fraught with social meaning as the British idiomatic convention of classes. If the explicit language of class is not to the forefront in perceptions of social divisions in the FRG, this can be accounted for by a number of contextual factors relating to the historical development of modern West Germany.

Geographical factors have played a role of considerable significance in militating against the formation of coherent classes and associate awareness, not least through the strength of the German federalist tradition. Territorial divisions—from the ant-hill absolutisms of the Holy Roman Empire, to the four zones of Allied occupation in 1945—together with migrational movement, have meant that the boundaries of the FRG's *Länder* correspond only approximately with historical ethnic differentiation. Nevertheless, each *Land* has retained and/or developed a certain degree of individual regional consciousness, manifested in styles of building, cuisine, custom, dialect and colloquial aphorisms about 'tribal' character.

More crucial, perhaps in undermining class concepts

generally was the phenomenon of East to West migration. Although there had been some tradition of this since the 1880s,[1] the population movement in consequence of Germany's defeat and political division was unprecedented. At the start of the Potsdam Conference in July 1945, 4 million Germans had already left their homelands in the eastern territories. With the Conference's decision for a 'transfer' of the German inhabitants of Poland, Czechoslovakia and Hungary, most of the 5.6 million Germans still living east of the Oder and Neisse rivers were expelled by force, as were some 3.5 million Sudeten Germans. Many died *en route*, and not all of them settled in the western zones, but by the end of 1961 (with the building of the Berlin Wall and the strengthening of security on FRG/GDR borders) over 12 million expellees had arrived in West Germany. Not only did the huge influx of *déclassés*—titled, but penniless *Junkers*, for example—exacerbate the already existing social dislocation; political division into two Republics also entailed West Germany losing the old heartlands of working-class consciousness, Berlin and Saxony. Overall, division, together with the geopolitical peculiarities of West Berlin, not only brought the issue of national identification into sharper focus, but also facilitated, within a Cold War climate, the discrediting of class-based ideologies. A further consideration is the Republic's lack of an undisputed metropolitan centre as the seat of 'good society', comparable to Paris or London: instead, cities such as Munich, Cologne or Düsseldorf have tended to develop their own 'top' set.

The significance of religion as an issue submerging class interests or, at least, providing an alternative focal point of social identification should also be noted. The Occupation years and the 1950s saw a marked upswing in what might be termed religiosity amongst the population of the western zones, expressed in increased church-going and in the attempt, through the founding of the CDU/CSU, to apply Christian principles to politics. Not least, both Churches commanded considerable respect amongst the Allied and civilian population on account of the exemplary courage of their leaders during Nazi persecution.

Following defeat, the overriding priority for most Germans was basic physical survival in appalling conditions of privation, described by one British eye-witness as follows:

Thousands of corpses still lying under the rubble of German towns produced a plague of rats and flies. In Berlin, an epidemic of malignant boils which necessitated immediate amputation of the infected part, produced a thousand hospital cases a day. Malnutrition and infected water brought typhoid, paratyphoid and dysentery. The Winter of 1946/47 was one of the coldest on record in Europe. In Berlin, two hundred people were recorded as 'frozen to death'. Western Germany, said ex-President Hoover, had sunk to a level of destitution, which had not been seen in Europe for a hundred years.[2]

Public belief that West Germany's subsequent economic recovery was 'miraculous' was based on a number of misconceptions, not least the assumption that the year 1945 represented 'Zero Hour'. The loss of industrial productive capacity in the western zones through war damage, territorial division and Allied dismantling only amounted to about 25 per cent of what had been, in any case, an exceptionally high war-time level. Whilst production levels did remain low until 1948, this was due more to a collapse of the infrastructure than to actual destruction of plant. Dismantling frequently brought the replacement of obsolescent machinery and proved beneficial in the long term; the western zones—later the FRG—contained over 61 per cent of the Reich's pre-war industrial capacity, and the influx of qualified refugees compensated for the skilled labour lost during the war. The Allies' policy of Currency Reform in 1948, whereby every adult received a total of 60 new DM, savings being exchanged at the rate of 10:1, generated a public ethos of 'putting everyone on the same footing'. Its ultimate effect, however, beyond ending the ubiquitous black market and barter system, was to place wealth distribution on an extremely unequal basis: large private fortunes were amassed, within several years, by those who owned plant or property etc., but average savers saw their cash assets virtually wiped out overnight. The Equalisation of Burdens Act of 1952 (exacting levies, payable over a 30-year period and amounting to half the value of all private assets held in 1948/49) in practice did little to further equality, partly because 1948/49 had been a very lean year, and partly because the funds took a long time to reach those who were in greatest need.

Under the 'social market economy', money remained a

central public preoccupation. With the transition from the hungry 1940s to the rising living standards and trend towards full employment of the 1950s, there occurred during the 1960s a shift of emphasis from primary needs, i.e. getting one's self and one's family fed, clothed and housed, towards the more 'prestigious'.

Given the overall rise in living standards, and thanks to the new availability of consumer goods, many West Germans were able to look, at least, middle-class, with public attention being diverted away from the fact that a chance for thorough-going economic reorganisation had evaporated.

Little reform has been effected in the field of education: the comprehensive school programme has only been partially introduced. Meanwhile, the system that historically had given a basic education to all, but advanced academic training to only a few, continues to operate on a traditional selective three-track pattern at secondary level (*Hauptschule, Mittelschule, Oberschule*). Children failing to be selected for entry into an intermediate school remain in the senior level of the primary school before attending part-time vocational training school (*Berufsschule*). Revealing is the 1965 decree, by the Baden-Württemberg *Landtag*, that the *Hauptschule* should also be known—along with the Intermediate and Upper (*Gymnasium*, i.e. grammar) schools—as '*weiterführend*', that is, leading on (to further studies). This represented perhaps a cosmetic attempt to hide the traditional implications that it does not lead anywhere. West German private schools, few in number, are associated less with academic excellence than with wealth or modish progressiveness. The traditional social prestige of the university graduate (*Akademiker*) is again not attached to specific universities—there are no West German counterparts to Oxford, Cambridge, Yale, Harvard, etc., nor the traditional/ redbrick distinction. Opinion research has for years indicated that the university professor is top of the career prestige scale— a modern manifestation of the respect accruing, in the eighteenth century, to the Estate of Learned Scholars (*der Gelehrtenstand*). As in France, distinctions are made within the teaching profession: prospective *Volksschullehrer* and *Mittelschullehrer* train at a *pädagogische Hochschule*, whilst university-trained *Gymnasium* teachers are titled, in accordance with the administrative grade of the civil service, in five ranks: *Studienassessor, Studienrat, Oberstudienrat, Studiendirektor, Oberstudiendirektor.* The social standing of degrees is illustrated not least in the widespread use of double titles—e.g. Herr/Frau Professor Doktor and Herr/Frau Doktor Doktor—and in poll figures for 1979 indicating that the prestige of *Akademiker* has not declined (and seems unlikely to do so in future).[3]

Konrad Adenauer once remarked, so the story goes, that West Germans are more interested in watching TV than in politics. Whilst it is true that actual party members (currently 5 per cent of the electorate) are vastly outnumbered by Thomas Mann's 'unpolitical Germans', general 'interest' in politics has risen steadily, since the late 1960s in particular,[4] and by both European and US standards, electoral turn-out is high, peaking at over 90 per cent for *Bundestag* elections. If the correlation between politics and social class is not, perhaps, as obvious as it is in Great Britain for example, this is probably due to two developments both important in terms of the erosion of class awareness: first, the 'privatisation' of politics, deriving from the Nazi experience and resulting in the fairly widespread attitude of '*ohne mich*' ('count me out'); secondly, the almost supra-ideological democratic fundamentalism preached by the CDU/CSU and—with its formal relinquishment of its historical commitment to Marxist goals, under the Godesberg Programme of 1959—the SPD, with promises of benefits for all sections of society, which helped to remove much of the class 'edge' from politics.

Finally, there is employment—a vital factor in the shaping of class conceptions. With regard to manual workers—still the largest occupational grouping in the FRG—certain specifically German developments are of significance. In contrast to Britain, for example, where common structures of working-class consciousness and culture were developing as early as the 1830s, the majority of German industrial workers were, even by 1914, still only first- or second-generation. Under Bismarck's Anti-Socialist Laws of 1878–90, the organised labour movement had been driven into a sub-cultural ghetto—a process repeated during the National Socialist regime. Under Hitler, the imperial official distinction between manual workers and salaried employees was abolished in favour of the terms *Arbeiter der Faust und Stirn*, literally workers by fist and forehead[5] and classes were declared to have ceased to exist, with propaganda being directed at a more abstract notion of working (but not working-class) people, e.g. *die Werktätigen, die Schaffenden*, or *die Arbeitnehmer*. During this period also, in line with neo-feudal doctrines of 'blood and soil', the *Bauer* (more like the French *paysan* than the English peasant)—a term of ridicule during the late nineteenth-century—underwent something of an ideological renaissance. After the collapse of the Third Reich, with subsequent agricultural reforms, however, the connotation of a horny-handed son of the soil has been removed by the official adoption of the more neutral label *Landwirt* (farmer).

Der Mittelstand, the middle estate, is a term still employed in a variety of social contexts, although it has no historical legal foundation. *Mittelstandspolitik* was the creation of late nineteenth-century politicians, and posited the existence of a united buffer between the poles of capital and labour, a saviour of the social order. Characterised, in reality, by fairly divergent life-styles and disparate economic interests, the uniformity of the *Mittelstand* existed mainly as a common anxiety to maintain the status quo. By the early twentieth century, distinction was made between an 'old' middle estate of economically independent artisans, agriculturalists and liberal professionals, and a rapidly-expanding 'new' wing of white-collar dependent clerical employees and technicians. The word *Bürger*, also traditionally associated with the middle classes, was used, at the time of the French Revolution, like *citoyen*, as a direct mode of address amongst democrats, later becoming a customary form of public address to the inhabitants of a town or state. Today, this survives in the shape of *Staatsbürger* and *Bundesbürger*. In its adjectival form, it has retained the meaning of 'non-aristocratic', although derogatory undertones have crept in: The French *bourgeois* acquired the German equivalents of *Besitzbürger, Kleinbürger* or, even worse, *Spiessbürger* (in medieval times, an honourable citizen who rushed to arms in defence of his town, but later a pious hypocrite or philistine). In short, the term *Bürger* has proved a willing beast of political burden: eighteenth-century revolutionary aspirations, nineteenth-century Conservative gentility and, in the twentieth century, it has connoted variously anything from a political reactionary, to a modern left-wing student participating in a protest action, a *Bürgerinitiative*.

If, in terms of industrial relations, attitudes do not appear as 'hard' as they do in Great Britain, this can be accounted for by a combination of relevant factors: the Nazi suppression of the trades union movement; the nature of the post-war Confederation of Trades Unions (the DGB, which, formally political neutral, pursuing, like its US counterpart the AFL/CIO, collective bargaining within the existing economic, social and political system, has no closed shop principle); the achievement during the early 1950s of limited worker-co-determination, lending, to some degree, the labour movement an air of being '*salonfähig*' or socially acceptable; the existence of over 2 million immigrant workers executing, as a rule, the lowest paid and least pleasant of manual tasks. All these explain, in some part, apparently low working-class militancy, though of course low strike levels can also say more about the strength of employer controls than about a possible absence of working-class awareness.

Official Images

For the majority of advanced societies, census categories, Acts of social legislation and governmental declarations generally represent a guide as to what social groupings are held, by the official mind, to be in existence. In the case of the Federal Republic, such official perceptions are of arguably greater significance than their counterparts in, say, Britain, France or the United States, in that they have not only to some degree determined actual 'life chances' during the period under consideration (via category-specific policy measures), but also coincide widely with the perceptions held in other quarters.

THE CENSUS

As in other countries, the West German census[6] reports on the gainfully employed in terms of economic branch[7] and individual occupational position (*Stellung im Beruf*). It is this latter set of categories which comes close to being a description of class as both an historical and a popularly understood phenomenon. Although there is no officially fixed sequence, the order in which the categories are customarily presented implicitly suggests a hierarchy:

a. 'Independents', i.e. self-employed (*Selbständige*), defined as including:

> 'those running a business whether in trade or agriculture, as an owner or lessee (*Pächter*). Of determining significance is economic independence. Also all those occupied in the liberal professions, such as doctors, writers, lawyers, artists etc.'
>
> 'private teachers, auditors, accountants, midwives . . . entrepreneurs, independent master-tradesmen, street traders, visiting seamstress'.[8]

Beyond the predominant criterion of economic independence, though, there are hints of some official recognition of social distinctions entailing prestige, rather than wealth or power. As in the French census, the term 'liberal professions', for example, is applied solely to those working on their own account 'with their own practice . . . but not to members of these professions who are only in a dependent position'.[9] Similarly, the 'independents' category also excludes 'those with a formal contract of employment who, within their field, are ultimately able to run the business as though it were their own, e.g. an independent branch manageress'[10] (who, presumably, enjoys greater power in the hiring and firing of staff than the actual owner).

b. In contrast to comparable societies, where they generally take on the official class of the family breadwinner (usually male), the spouses and families of agricultural and non-agricultural owners in Germany have, by tradition, been accorded a census category of their own: 'Assisting Family Members' (*mithelfende Familienangehörige*), provided that they are not in receipt of any payment for their services to the head (or other member) of the family.

c. 'Officials' (*Beamte*) are defined as 'those in possession of a certificate calling them into public service, administrative or technical, but not in permanent or temporary retirement' (in 1950), or (in 1970) as 'officials of the Federal State, of the *Länder*, of the parishes or other bodies of public law, including probationers, also clerics of the churches in Germany belonging to the Evangelical Church and of the Roman Catholic Church'.[11] Official recognition of the traditional prestige accorded to the bearer of the title *Beamte* is apparent in the emphatic exclusion of 'persons using the title "insurance official" or "bank official" without being in the service of a corporation under public laws'.[12]

d. '(Salaried) Employees' (*Angestellte*) and defined largely in terms of compulsory pension insurance schemes (see below), as including 'leading employees' (*leitende Angestellte*) (managers, confidential clerks and authorised agents), so-called 'insurance and banking officials', together with trainees in commercial, technical and administrative occupations. There are again hints of official assumptions about social status implicit in the fact that *Hausangestellte* (female domestic servants) are not classed as *Angestellte* since the majority of them come under the worker pension scheme, the exceptions thus being known as 'housekeepers-in-charge' (*Hausdamen*—literally, 'houseladies'—with a definite ring of gentility to it!).[13] At the same time, however, pension affiliation is overridden in the case of foremen (*Werkmeister*), deemed (presumably in recognition of their supervisory function) by the census to be *Angestellte*, as are those workers to whom, after faithful service, the contract status of *Angestellte* has been accorded.[14]

e. 'Workers' (*Arbeiter*). These are all wage-earners who, until 1970, were stated to be 'almost exclusively covered by the compulsory Workers' Insurance Scheme' and (from 1961, in recognition of changing patterns of remuneration) 'irrespective of the periods of wage payment and assessment'.[15] Again, as with the French census, distinction is made not on the basis of skill, but along the manual–non-manual line, though these terms are not actually used. Explicitly included in all these censuses are 'homeworkers (*Heimarbeiter*), and home helps (*Hausgehilfen*)'. Apprentices (*Lehrlinge*), classed in the 1950 census as *Arbeiter*, had by 1970 acquired two separate categories of their own, rather less feudal in tone: 'Trainees (*Auszubildende*) in recognised commercial and technical training occupations' and 'trainees in recognised training trades'.[16]

INSURANCE AND OTHER SOCIAL LEGISLATION

The German system of statutory social insurance, introduced towards the end of the nineteenth century, consolidated during the Wilhelmine and Weimar periods, and ultimately resurrected (largely unaltered) after the collapse of the Nazi régime, accounts particularly for the divisions felt, both officially and unofficially, to split German society into broad classes. Since the time of Bismarck, criticism of the separate provisions[17] for different sections of the population had been voiced by the trades unions, by the SPD and by the KPD in particular, who called for universal cover and standardisation. Despite the drafting of reform proposals in 1946/47 by the Manpower Directorate of the Allied Control Commission (influenced in part by British developments following the Beveridge Report of 1942), and despite (or perhaps because of) the ratification of these proposals within the Soviet zone of occupation, the system of social insurance (most notably pensions) remained unreformed. Predictably, self-interest prompted private insurance companies, the independent medical profession and employers to oppose the principle of universality.[18]

Pension insurance legislation in the Federal Republic is based on the Reich Insurance Act of 1911—a fusion of the Invalidity and Old Age Security Act (1889) and the newly-enacted Salaried Employees Pension Law (AVG). Neither Act provides a legally binding definition of 'worker' or of 'salaried employee', but both offer non-exhaustive catalogues of (manual) occupation,[19] whilst the *AVG* expressly, if tautologically, covers:

[para 2] . . . all salaried employees, apprentice and trainee salaried employees, independent teachers, tutors, musicians not themselves employing any salaried employees; independent artistes; midwives with permits to practice; independents active in the care of the sick, in maternity, infant and child care, not employing any salaried employees; marine pilots; members of spiritual cooperatives (*Genossenschaften*), deaconesses, German Red Cross nurses and members of similar communities engaged in the care of the sick, teaching or in other non profit-making activities for predominantly religious or moral motives; persons performing a voluntary social year.

[para 3] The following, in particular, belong to the salaried employees:

1. salaried employees in a managerial position,
2. technical salaried employees in firms, offices and administration, foremen and other salaried employees in a similarly elevated or senior position (*gehobenen oder höheren Stellung*),
3. office salaried employees, provided that they are not engaged exclusively in messenger, cleaning, tidying and similar tasks, including workshop clerks,
4. shop assistants and other salaried employees in commercial (*Handlungsgehilfen*) services, even if the object of the enterprise is not a trading concern, assistants and trainees in chemists,
5. members of stage companies and musicians, irrespective of the artistic value of their performances,
6. salaried employees in occupations of education, teaching, welfare, care of the sick, charity care,
7. ships' helmsmen, deck and engineering service officers, ships' doctors, radio officers, pursers, administrators and administrative assistants and similarly elevated and senior members of the crews of inland ships or German seafaring vessels,
8. civil aircraft personnel.[20]

Both the existence of, and the conditions for, the two separate schemes mark out a stark manual/non-manual divide. Indeed, the fact that worker 'invalidity' comes under the pension, rather than health insurance, scheme is itself a relic of the nineteenth-century official notion of its being the natural fate of workers to become 'used up', as it were. Similarly, although in 1948 the widows of workers were for the first time granted an unconditional pension, reserved hitherto to the widows of salaried employees only, they received a lower rate, the assumption being, no doubt, that they were more likely to be going out to earn a living in any case. Workers' invalidity, traditionally the loss of one-third of the ability to work, contrasts with the salaried employees' 'incapacity to pursue an occupation' (*Berufsunfähigkeit*), set at 50 per cent (though both levels were aligned at 50 per cent in 1948). Moreover, for salaried employees, 'capacity to pursue an occupation' expressly excluded having to retrain for an 'alien' (*berufsfremd*) job, a privilege which in 1956 both government and opposition acknowledged as being unjust.[21] Proposals for a unified Pension Act met with tremendous protest from the DAG, the salaried employees' union, whose shrill publicity campaign (featuring headlines such as 'Major Alarm For All Of Us!', a petition carrying over 800,000 signatures and the sending of a real tomahawk, as a symbolic declaration of war, to Chancellor Adenauer)[22] in part contributed to the retention of separate pension schemes.

Although savings, as a provision for retirement, have been proved historically to be a hazardous business in Germany (1923 inflation, Currency Reform of 1948), official thinking was remarkably slow in surrendering the old-style distinction between feckless workers and responsible salaried employees: it was only in 1968 that pension insurance was made compulsory also for all salaried employees, irrespective of income level. Furthermore, separate pension arrangements for mining employees (*Arbeiter* and *Angestellte*) under the *Knappschaft* system (the guild-like associations dating from the thirteenth century, codified in 1923) indicate an official view of pitmen as a community all of their own.

It would seem that an image of a quasi-feudal society, characterised by ideals of independence, thrift and estate-separateness, with self-help as the key to a comfortable bourgeois living prevented the extension of compulsory insurance to the self-employed. As Economics Minister Erhard put it in 1956:

As a rule, there is property involved, usually in the form of industrial plant, which represents in itself a considerable reserve. There is also the fact that, in periods of labour shortage, craftsmen and peasant-farmers can usually rely on members of the family or even outsiders to keep the business going, and old people inevitably find a comfortable living in the bosom of the family, even after they have handed over their business or farm.[23]

Gradually, though, the image of one solid grouping of 'independents' becomes more fragmented: by 1957, farmers were granted their own compulsory protection under the 'Law on Old Age Assistance for Farmers'; from 1962, self-employed craftsmen were deemed to come under the workers' compulsory scheme, whilst sections of the 'liberal professions' were granted admission to the *Angestellten* scheme on a voluntary basis (and, in the case of artists, journalists, writers and musicians, on a compulsory basis, under the 'Artists Social Insurance Act' of 1 January 1983), or came under the terms of special plans varying from *Land* to *Land*.[24]

Once again, the old 'estate' characteristic stands out quite starkly in the plethora of health insurance schemes, with agricultural sickness funds (*Landwirtschaftliche Krankenkassen*) for independent farmers and their families, guild funds (*Innungskrankenkassen*) for independent craftsmen and their employees, as well as separate societies for miners (*Knappschaften*). A fundamental official distinction has persisted between workers and salaried employees, not only in that the former are without exception liable to compulsory insurance, and the latter only within a certain income limit, but also in the fact that it was not until 1970 that workers received up to six weeks' full wages during illness, an entitlement enjoyed by *Angestellten* since 1930. That the spectre of the illicitly absent worker loomed large in the official mind seems apparent from the fact that, until 1970, benefit was still withheld for the first day of sickness.[25]

Legislation regarding contracts of employment and industrial relations recognises a basic division between employers (*Arbeitgeber*—work-givers) and the employed (*Arbeitnehmer*—work-takers). The latter term, first used in the

Trading Regulations of 1869, originally denoted manual workers, but was gradually applied to *Angestellten* as well; its usage after the Second World War recalls in part the Nazi precept of the 'unity' of 'workers by brain and workers by fist'. Given the inconsistencies in its use in various official sources,[26] it is not surprising to find 'work-takers' customarily subdivided into salaried employees and workers, by reference to the pension laws. Acts relating to co-determination and works' constitutions express a similar 'work-giver' and 'work-taker' dichotomy, with the latter again sub-divided, although the 1976 Law on Co-Management provides for work-taker seats to be distributed amongst 'workers, salaried employees, trades union representatives and one managerial salaried employee (*leitender Angestellte*)'. The latter's presence as an official representative of the work-takers' camp, as it were, has been a matter of some contention with trades unionists in particular, the argument being that the *leitender Angestellte* has a greater community of interest with owners and employers than with other work-takers. The qualitative distinction officially made between workers and salaried employees is also apparent in other areas of employment legislation: *Angestellte* are accorded a minimum of six weeks' basic notice; workers, however, being regarded as more dispensable, are granted a minimum period of only two weeks before being thrown to the mercy of the general labour market.[27] Some blurring of the traditional *Arbeiter/Angestellte* distinction has taken place: for example, the old class-based assumption behind remuneration rulings for workers (i.e. living from hand to mouth, unable to manage unless paid weekly) has given way to the possibility of monthly payment. None the less, the fact that these earnings are termed 'monthly wages', as distinct from 'salary', looks remarkably like the use of a status differential as a means of keeping the workers 'in their place'. *Beamte* receive a special kind of salary (*Dienstbezüge*) based not on the principle of remuneration for services rendered, but instead on a traditional pension (*Rente*), comprising a basic graded salary (*Grundgehalt*) and various additional allowances, enabling them to maintain a living 'befitting their estate' (*standesgemäss*).[28]

Welfare provisions are an indication of who, in the official mind, is perceived as having needs over and above the statutory provisions available to the population as a whole, thus identifying a possible underclass. From 1924 onwards, welfare legislators had no longer recognised the social plight customarily associated with the proletariat and lumpenproletariat (i.e. poverty—*Armut*), but instead that of 'being in need of assistance' (*Hilfsbdürftigkeit*). The fact that this somewhat broader definition was retained under the traditional principle of 'welfare' (*Fürsorge*, from the verb 'to take care of') by the authors of the Federal Basic Law indicates official recognition of the range of predicaments (homelessness, undernourishment, loss of all material possessions, quite apart from straightforward financial hardship), to which, through military defeat, Allied occupation, and geographical division, a vast (and socially heterogeneous) number of people had fallen victim.

By 1961, however, with the bulk of the immediate crises associated with post-war social dislocation overcome, 'welfare' was replaced, under a new Act, by 'social assistance' (*Sozialhilfe*), while 'those in need of assistance' (*Hilfsbedürftige*) became 'assistance recipients' (*Hilfeempfänger*). This represented not solely an official attempt to eradicate the social stigma attached to the old terms,[29] but also a modification of the old-style image of inevitable helpless and needy masses; greater emphasis was lent to the exceptional, the individual and the active aspects.

Behind the niceties of terms such as 'the endangered, who lack the inner consolidation to lead an orderly life', or 'persons with particular social difficulties', lies a grouping of largely *disparate* elements, including the long-term mentally and physically handicapped, the chronically alcoholic and 'above all, the homeless, persons of no fixed abode, gypsies, vagrants and released prisoners',[30] frequently summarised as 'marginal strata'.

What conclusions may be drawn regarding an official view of West German society? Clearly, there is no explicit reference made to class as *Klasse*, the letter of the law being in line with the democratic fundamentalism proclaimed, for example by the Republic's Basic Law, e.g. 'No person may be advantaged or disadvantaged on account of their sex, origin, race, language, homeland, background [*Herkunft*], faith, religious or political beliefs.'[31] Its spirit is somewhat different, however, in that ultimate *inequality* is condoned in the Basic Law's precept of the 'free unfolding of personality'—the legal justification of the ideology of West Germany as an 'achievement society'. Somewhat paradoxically, social policy under CDU/CSU/FDP coalition government largely perpetuated material and status distinctions along lines approximating to classes, best summarised by the census (occupational position) categories *Arbeiter/Angestellte/Beamte/Selbständige*, at a time when in the arena of public debate, the very existence of classes was being denied (or at least, masked) by the ideal of a broad 'middle-estate' society. From the late 1960s onwards, however, just as the concept of class was in the process of acquiring wider political and public currency, policy measures were being enacted to level off some, though not all, class-based social inequality.[32] As in other countries, an upper class tends to escape from official perceptions, but the term '*Unternehmer*' (entrepreneur) is often applied to large-scale owners, in particular. In this respect, interesting evidence is presented in a series of articles on the 'images of the social partners', published by the Federal Government Press and Information Office in 1953:

For many of the middle estate and for many entrepreneurs, the worker is still—subconsciously and subliminally—the eternally discontented proletarian who comes from 'lower down', who wears a red tie, sings the 'Internationale' at inapproriate moments, quotes Marx and prepares for the dictatorship of the proletariat. He is 'of course' a trades union member, votes Communist or Socialist, lives in a slum area and has a lot of children. . . . The truth looks different: the worker, to judge by his standard of living, at any rate, has long since moved up into the stratum which, in former times, one would have termed the 'middle estate'. Many qualified, skilled workers live and are housed better than civil servants, salaried employees or academically trained members of the liberal professions. They are well clothed, have variously their own little house and often a motorbike, they go on holiday trips and send their children—if they are gifted—to university. Nevertheless, a vestige of the old historically-determined 'class consciousness' often still lives on in some of them. They frequently feel proletarian—with no external reason—but they live in a thoroughly bourgeois (*bürgerlich*) fashion. Conversely, many members of the old middle estate are impoverished today, and often live more modestly than do many workers, though they still feel part of a bourgeoisie (*Bürgertum*) . . .

After this discussion of the 'image' of the worker, there follows an examination of the 'distorted image' (*Zerrbild*) of the entrepreneur:

For many people, but for many workers especially, the entrepreneur, seen from an entirely emotional viewpoint, is still the 'capitalist': living off inherited or ill-gotten money which he uses to build factories in which workers—deprived of all rights and property—are exploited, whilst he himself lives magnificently and joyfully off his huge profits and tax evasions. The luxury limousine is just as much a part of this image as is the vast villa in which glittering parties are held, with the champagne flowing in rivers.[33]

The continuing existence of such class distinctions is suggested not least by the similar social groupings which were identified by Chancellor Helmut Kohl, for example, in his 1982 call for 'solidarity extending beyond all groups and social barriers': 'I appeal . . . to trades unions and to employers [*Arbeitgeber*], to industry and to middle-estate trade, to workers, to salaried employees, to civil servants, members of the liberal professions, craftsmen and to peasants . . .'[34] Tautological as many of the official sources are, it is possible to sense an implicit social hierarchy. Noticeably, the images of this hierarchy suggest that, whilst the lower level divisions are apparently perceived in a fairly unequivocal and undifferentiated manner, those higher up are more problematical and correspondingly less precise. The overall picture is therefore not unlike that suggested by French official sources,[35] i.e. a distinctive and clearly-defined class of workers, with a somewhat variegated range of middle classes situated above them.

Academic Images

Official images of West German society have been marked, as we have seen, by a distinct absence of explicit reference to *Klassen*, and within social scientific debate of the postwar period, a similar trend is observable until the late sixties at least. If contemporary commentators in Britain, for example, had become rather less inhibited about 'discussing the nasty subject in good company',[36] and in France the subject of class reverberated with a significance that was political, rather than purely intellectual, virtually opposite tendencies were typical of West German scholarship during the 1950s and early 1960s. Clearly, this was in part a result of twelve years of National Socialist dictatorship during which all discussion of class was officially suppressed. Indeed, even prior to the *Machtergreifung*, 'the language and ideas of class struggle were as discredited amongst the best people in scholarly research as they were amongst the best people in politics', as one leading Weimar sociologist observed.[37] After 1945, therefore, when the ideological climate regarding matters such as the Cold War, economic, social and political reconstruction was much influenced by the model of the United States, certain parallels were also apparent in the academic treatment of class. A kind of democratic fundamentalism was the thrust behind the almost autosuggestive formula that the concept of class was an outdated one.

The concept of 'social strata' appeared more acceptable within the forum of sociological debate, not only in its freedom from the odium of Marxism, but also in its multi-dimensional, more 'modern' applicability under a constellation of rather special historical circumstances. Widespread processes of social mobility—upward, in the case of industrial workers and, to a more individual degree, technical and administrative salaried employees, downward in the case of the old bourgeoisie of property and education (*Besitz- und Bildungsbürgertum*)— dating from the end of the First World War but accelerating after 1945 in particular—accounted, in the view of Helmut Schelsky, for the formation of a 'relatively uniform social stratum, no more proletarian than it is bourgeois'.[38] According to this theory, introduced in 1953, with the levelling of 'real economic and political status', social and cultural forms of behaviour had become standardised into a 'petty-bourgeois/ middle-estate lifestyle . . . whereby uniform participation in the material and spiritual comforts of civilisation . . . can permit almost everyone to develop a sense of no longer being right "at the bottom" [*unten*]'.[39]

An undifferentiating emphasis on consumer behaviour and mass-society life-style as a leveller of classes became typical of many academic statements during the 1950s.[40] There was much discussion of the worker becoming 'socially integrated', yet much of the source evidence—ranging in tone from the condescending, e.g. 'workers are astonishingly receptive towards cultural values',[41] to the moralistic, e.g. 'their income may well have become "bourgeois", but their manner of spending it (H.P.) is still "proletarian" '[42]—suggests that class distinctions were still perceived, though not admitted.

Several empirical studies of Federal society as a whole were published during the 1950s and early 1960s, using stratification schemes involving a variety of criteria derived, in the main, from occupation. Schelsky made an important contribution to academic debate in opening up discussion on the significance of subjective factors: like Centers before him, he argued that:

the class reality of our present society is scarcely to be found in real, economic and social class situations, but it is still widely present as *class consciousness* . . . and class consciousness is just as much a social reality determining people's behaviour as is an economic, political, legal etc. class situation.[43]

Relative social prestige, defined largely via Warner's methodology of 'social self-stratification', thus figured widely in the models presented during this period.[44] Overall, these posited the existence of a very thin upper stratum (*Oberschicht*) above a broad middling grouping comprising subsections of the middle and lower strata.

It was an American sociologist, Morris Janowitz, who had thus identified these 'broadly defined social strata, or if you will, social classes'[45] within Federal German society in 1955. Subsequent studies often reproduced his categories:

		%
Upper-middle:	Professionals, managers and proprietors of larger establishments, and upper civil servants	4.6
Lower-middle:	Minor officials, clerical and sales persons, small businessmen, and independent artisans, farmers	38.6
Upper-lower:	Skilled workers and employed artisans	13.3
Lower-lower:	Semi-skilled and unskilled workers, farmworkers	38.6
Unclassifiable:	(including social security pensioners):	4.9

Happily, Janowitz's somewhat questionable inclusion, on the basis of size alone, of 'the very small percentage (less than 1 per cent) who might be classified within the upper stratum'[46] within the upper-middle stratum, was not emulated by his West German colleagues. Thus, for example, Moore and

Kleining ascribed large proprietors, large landowners, the nobility and holders of prestigious positions in politics, economics, finance and law (1 per cent in their 1960 study) to a separate upper stratum (*Oberschicht*), with Bolte and Kappe, as well as Scheuch identifying an *Oberschicht* comprising 2 per cent of the population.[47]

Similarly, Moore and Kleining's separate category for the very bottom of society, the 'socially despised' (*Sozial Verachtete*)—labourers, casual workers such as odd-jobbers (*Handlanger*), seasonal workers, day-labourers, unskilled workers such as newspaper deliverers, and workers on very dirty jobs, 4 per cent of their sample—also features in research findings by others.[48]

Diversity—in methodology (descriptive/analytical approach), criteria (inclusion/exclusion of subjective factors), terminology and, not least, in overall findings (size and number of strata)—of these early models prompted Ralf Dahrendorf to conclude 'that in present-day German society [mid-1960s] there are no social strata which are so unequivocally distinctive that each observer is bound to identify them'.[49] Whether or not this was an over-statement of the case, it seems at any rate certain that, conversely, few members of a putative 'upper-lower non-industrial stratum', for example, would actually recognise (let alone refer to) themselves as such.[50] In this respect, Dahrendorf's own stratification scheme for the Federal Republic does less violence to German colloquial usage in that he takes into account certain historical forces shaping both collective consciousness (cf. Geiger's *Schichtmentalität*) and the colloquial usage itself.

Published in 1968, Dahrendorf's model[51] depicted West German society divided, as he put it, 'like a house with seven rooms', into the following strata:

1. a small, multiple élite consisting of less than 1 per cent of the population, lacking all consciousness of belonging to an upper statum or élite, even;
2. the 'service class' (*Dienstklasse*) of mainly non-technical civil servants and administrative salaried employees of all levels, encompassing 'that part of the new middle estate which is bureaucratically active', and possessed of a collective 'bureaucratic mentality' (12 per cent);
3. 'middle estate' i.e. the 'old middle estate', of independents, ranging from the 'liberal professions to small peasant farmers and retail traders,

including also independent entrepreneurs in industry', generally 'isolationist and defensive' in attitude (20 per cent);

4. a 'worker élite' of skilled workers who count themselves as belonging to the middle estate (5 per cent);

5. a 'false middle estate' of *Arbeiter*, nominally *Angestellte* within the tertiary industries, such as the waiter and the salesgirl, the conductor and the postman, the chauffeur and the petrol pump attendant who, because they work with people, are inclined to think of themselves as *mittelständisch* (12 per cent);

6. a 'worker stratum' which, although differentiated, has 'its own culture and mentality' (45 per cent); and, lastly,

7. a 'lower stratum' of socially despised elements, or 'Lumpenproletariat, . . . of long-term work-evaders, drifters, habitual offenders, and semi-literates' with no common mentality (5 per cent).

As far as mobility between the strata is concerned, Dahrendorf argued the existence of two medium-sized barriers, one 'between the élites and the adjoining areas of the service class and the middle estate, the other running between the lower stratum and the adjoining lower reaches of the worker stratum and false middle estate'. A third barrier, however, running from the lower end of the service class along the line dividing the worker stratum from the middle estate, was what Dahrendorf perceived as most insurmountable:

It divides an Above (*Oben*) from a Below (*Unten*), i.e. the upper third from the lower two-thirds of the stratification building. . . . German society continues to be a divided (*halbierte*, literally 'halved') society, cut up into an Above that knows little of the Below, and a Below that knows little of the Above.

This conclusion was not in itself startlingly novel: during the 1950s and 1960s,[52] sociological enquiry yielded fairly broad agreement with Popitz's findings that 'the industrial worker always sees society as divided into two . . . irrespective of whether he resignedly accepts it as an inevitable dichotomy, or whether he criticises it as a class society . . . "The other side" is, to him, obviously a great Unknown'.[53] Whilst Popitz had hinted that this dichotomous consciousness, determined not by ownership/non-ownership of the means of production, but by a manual/non-manual labour division, might be rooted in other social sources, sociologists such as Pross, in 1958, and Grimm, in 1966, related it directly to the question of educational qualification. They identified 'invisible, psychological barriers'[54] and 'informational and emotional distances'[55] to account for low worker-participation in higher education, which, of course, itself perpetuates the kind of mutual class prejudice that Dahrendorf apostrophised thus:

Just as the well-brought-up young lady (*höhere Tochter*) supposes every unshaven worker to be a potential sex-offender, so also do workers associate higher schooling with shadowy—albeit vague—notions of menace.[56]

Although the economic, social and political constellation had, until the late 1960s, done little to promote the articulation of Marxian class-based social analysis, there had, of course, been some who had swum against the tide of academic orthodoxy, as it were, but they were few in number. Paul Jostock, for example, in 1959 himself admitted the apparent futility of posing his question 'Is There Still a Proletariat?' since, as he correctly recognised, the very concept had largely come to denote what was once termed *Lumpenproletariat* or 'pauperism'.[57] The size and precise constitution of the *Arbeiterklasse* remained a key focus of Marxist theoretical debate, but when, after the census of 1970, class models of West German society as a whole began to be published, it seemed apparent that it was not just this class about which a consensus of opinion was problematic. Thus, for example, whilst Tjaden-Steinhauer and Tjaden arrived at a working population percentage figure of 83.3 per cent for the 1970 *Arbeiterklasse* of workers and the majority of salaried employees and civil servants, with a *Kapitalistenklasse* (owners, managers and other political, social and cultural rulers) of 1.8 per cent,[58] the Frankfurt Institute of Marxist Studies and Research (IMSF) gave figures of 75.6 per cent and 2.1 per cent respectively,[59] and for the year 1975, the *Projekt Klassenanalyse* group (PKA) offered 64.5 per cent and 4.6 per cent.[60]

Between the two 'major' and 'basic' classes (*Haupt-, Grundklassen*) are situated, in all three studies, a multiple middle grouping, termed variously 'non- or semi-capitalist special groups and strata', 'middle strata' and 'intermediate/ middle classes'.[61] Predictably, the class position of the *leitende Angestellte* (managerial salaried employees) was problematical, since their delegated function could be counted as part of productive labour, thereby making them wage-workers. At the same time, though, their 'wage' includes a premium beyond the value of their actual labour (in effect, a 'share in profit'), so this factor here determines their membership in the ranks of 'functioning' (*fungierenden*) capitalists. Again, the boundary between the middle and capitalist classes—being largely a matter of interpreting Marx's 'amount of surplus value in excess of normal wages'—is conveniently flexible. Thus, for example, whilst the IMSF determined that capitalist enterprise required a minimum of ten employees, the PKA set the boundary at five—a procedure that clearly has repercussions on both the size and the constitution of their capitalist class, which would accordingly embrace individuals of highly differentiated life chances, awareness, etc.

Marxist observers were, of course, not alone in experiencing some difficulty in identifying, with any great precision, the uppermost level of Federal German society—'a mysterious Unknown' to sociologists and to the public alike, as Pross commented in 1958.[62] The object of separate investigation by 'bourgeois' sociologists, from the 1960s,[63] the upper stratum (*Oberschicht*) (being the term almost invariably used in such studies) was generally agreed to be in some way 'new', relatively small (i.e. not greater than 5 per cent of the population), disparate in composition and therefore lacking in uniform awareness. With the aid of (somewhat self-conscious, one feels) sideways glances at the example of Britain, there has been repeated assertion that—because the upper stratum comprises various functional élites—there is no Establishment in the Federal Republic. Dahrendorf, of course, contributed towards the fragmenting of an Establishment image with his 'quasi-groups' (prestige upper stratum, economic upper stratum and ruling class or power élite), and with the distinction made between administrative, military, church, cultural, communications, economic and political élites. Despite fairly broad recognition that wealth, power and prestige do not necessarily coincide, some common characteristics of the *Oberschicht* have nevertheless been suggested:

Its members, as a rule, hold the highest positions in the field of occupation, they have the best educational training, they receive the highest income. Thus it can be expected of them that they can 'afford' the most, i.e. their own houses, large and comfortably furnished flats etc.[64]

Whilst noble lineage might, *prima facie*, be discounted as an automatic passport to the top, sociologists have by no means ruled out the continuing significance of social background in an allegedly 'open' or classless society.[65] The models which they have presented differ, according to the number of stratification variables, in shape and size, though occupation has retained its primary function. Some realistic pointers towards the social structure of the Federal Republic are provided: the shrinking of the old *Junker* and independent *Mittelstand* sectors and the expansion of dependent 'new' middle strata; stability of a small (i.e. up to 5 per cent) upper stratum not always entirely distinguishable from the upper reaches of the middle strata; the existence of a broadish aggregation (be it termed *Mittelstand* with the lasting overtones of an estate, or *Mittelschicht* or *Mittelklasse*); and reasonable numerical stability of a distinctive 'lower' stratum of predominantly waged/manual workers, beneath which (or possibly within, at its lowest reaches) are the marginal 'socially despised' elements constituting a *Lumpenproletariat* (though in the PKA study, the latter sits within the ranks of the *Mittelklasse*!). Their apparent smallness (about 5 per cent) would not seem, however, to take into account West Germany's immigrant workers or even the long-term victims of structural unemployment. Viewed overall, the countours suggested by academic testimony are of a society which is neither polarised into two classes, nor levelled out completely into one (or no class at all), but which—with its 'tendency towards the middle'—must comprise at least three classes in the broadest sense.

Informal Images

Whilst sociologists have deliberated whether, in the face of the complexity of stratification variables and increasing occupational differentiation, there is such a thing as '*the worker*', informal evidence from West Germany leaves little doubt that the concept continues to be applied by all sectors of society, to connote the same group of persons who are known, in official terminology, as *Arbeiter*. That the term—used, with perhaps greatest consistency and frequency by workers

137

themselves—is a symbolic expression of a life-position beyond the purely juridical, is illustrated not only by the manner in which it is colloquially employed in contexts wider than that of the workplace alone, but also by the frequency of the singular form *der Arbeiter*, emphasising a collective and uniform identity. Characteristic of the working-class self-image is a dichotomous mode of expression, although—as is in the very nature of subjective perceptions—uncertainty (as regards both the names applied to, and the precise location of the boundary felt to divide the two societal camps) tends to blur the picture. At times it would appear that the 'them/us' division is drawn somewhere above the official *Arbeiter/Angestellte* line, most noticeably during the early years of general privation. That hardship and bitterness was rightly perceived as being the preserve of not just the workers alone is apparent from the following. A woman signing herself 'a harassed, poor housewife with two greedy men to feed' protested against food shortages in 1947, concluding: 'The mug [*der Dumme*] is always the *Arbeiter* and the small *Angestellte*, he is the only one who obediently works for a couple of useless scraps of paper which won't buy him anything.'[66]

With the Currency Reform of 1948 having exacerbated the plight of the already-poor, have-nots, or 'little men' (although overall living standards did improve during the 1950s), the dichotomous focus persisted: many, generally unskilled and semi-skilled, workers felt that they had been 'forgotten' in the land of the economic miracle. Skilled workers, whilst acknowledging, for example, that 'we can afford the occasional glass of wine or beer, or a trip to the cinema or theatre, and some even manage a holiday', registered that 'nearly every self-employed person drives a car. The best that we can manage is a motorbike, bought by living from hand to mouth'.[67] It is striking how much reference is made, in workers' testimony, to the car: acting as a symbolic division between 'them and us' and an object of aspiration during the 1950s, and as a focus of an awareness, from the 1960s onwards, that they were in some way begrudged a rightful share in the fruits of prosperity.

A retired female worker, moved to verse by the plight of the 'simple man of labour' with his 'scant wage', wrote in 1962:

> And when the worker does own a car
> Then the *Herrn* kick up a fuss
> The sacrifices which he makes for it
> Are all one and the same to them, it's not
> down on their records . . .[68]

That she spoke for others, too, is clear from similar indignation typically voiced by 'a simple citizen', by 'us working people' and by 'a very small man on the street',[69] after Economics Minister Erhard's 1962 radio appeal for 'restraint' (*Mass haltung*) in the matter of wage claims. Generally speaking, prior to the beginnings of greater labour militancy around 1969, the informal testimony of (mostly unorganised) workers indicates the existence of vaguely resentful awareness of being different from the rich. A flower-seller, for instance, spoke of 'standing by their table, like a beggar, with the blood running to my head, not from anger, but from embarrassment.[70] The significance of money as a determining factor in workers' social self-images, has persisted into the 1970s. Evidence suggests that this social distinction—with all its attendant stereotypes of 'caviar' and 'Mercedes'[71]—is more readily understood than abstract notions of 'state monopoly capitalists'. This is well illustrated by the comments made to a student, anxious to get the discussion away from money, by a group of workers in 1974: 'But for us everything has to do with money! . . . Yes, you lot are always using such nice phrases about the dependent wage-earners, but that's us!'[71] A sense of manual labour as 'real' work is also typical, although notions of what is involved at the highest levels of white-collar activity are, in the main, vague, often verging on the obtuse: 'they have nothing to do all day other than sign papers . . . they don't need to work at all, less than a rag-and-bone man walking the streets crying "rags, bones, paper" '.[72] The more precise images which workers may have of lower-level administrative and clerical personnel suggest particular sensitivity to the *Arbeiter/Angestellte* division: 'They don't work as hard as we do. Whenever we go into their offices, they're always making personal telephone calls and are doing very little work.)[73] A sense of social stigma is apparent from reiterations of the white/blue theme:

139

Dirty hands, blue coat [*Kittel*]—that says it all. The blue coat alone advertises the fact. Workers are always viewed as second-class people. It hurts you that this distinction is made. In the canteen, too, we blue-coats are separated from the white-coats as though we were infectious or something.[74]

Outside the workplace, however, some workers have claimed—during the prosperous 1960s particularly—that 'people no longer notice who is a worker and who is a clerical employee'.[75] A skilled painter spoke for many when he emphasised how he 'set great store by looking tip-top when I go out, no one is supposed to recognise that I am a worker when they see me out',[76] and a steelworker boasted of being indistinguishable from an entrepreneur 'when I'm all got up and immaculate, standing the rounds'.[77] This unmistakable sense of achievement at *hiding*, rather than altering, their status indicates a generally low level of class pride amongst German workers at that time, and gives grounds for supposing that for many, being a worker meant being under a 'life sentence', whereby 'progress' could be equated with simply success at disguise. Associated with this is the idea of language as a significant social distinction: informal testimony over a wide period suggests recognition, by workers, of a distinct barrier, coinciding, more or less, with the *Arbeiter/Angestellte* divide. Thus, for example, miners were recorded as being reluctant to 'speak out in front of clerical employees' at meetings,[78] whilst a former factory girl collaborating with students, social workers and workers on a book about 'social' housing in West Berlin noted how workers 'couldn't keep up with the style of the so-called "intellectuals"—as we used to call anyone who was not a worker'.[79] Another member of the group, a decorator, firmly believed that 'the way someone talks tells you about where they stand in society'. By writing the book in High German (*Hochdeutsch*), he argued:

you'll be giving a completely distorted picture because linguistically it will sound like someone from grammar school. The reader, confused, won't know what to think: Is that a worker, then, who stands right at the bottom of society, simply a servant? Or is it someone who's had schooling and who's turned into an idiot later?[80]

Awareness of a division between basic and 'higher' education is a strikingly consistent feature of workers' testimony: *Angestellte*, *Beamte* and *Akademiker* (graduates) are widely regarded as preferring to remain socially 'within their own circles', their oft-criticised snobbery, '*Standesdünkel*' (literally, estate-arrogance), being attributed, typically, to the fact that 'a man with no learning is treated as a second- or third-class person.[81] 'The worker is stupid' is a frequent and ambiguous motif, conveying resignation or, on occasions, deliberate irony, with the suggestion of 'the worker is a fool *to put up with all that he does*'.

Characteristic of statements by salaried employees is an emphasis on being socially and culturally superior to manual workers, even though, by the 1960s, sections of the latter were often financially better off. The phantom of the 'thousand-mark worker' loomed large in the mind of the salaried employee: 'There are five worker families living in my house', wrote the wife of a minor *Angestellter*, 'and as one of the small, conscientious savers who, in their restraint and moderation, form the cornerstone of the State, I am constantly horrified at the way in which they senselessly squander their money'.[82] Values such as thrift and diligence frequently permit dependent salaried employees to ascribe themselves to the 'middle estate'. Historically, and colloquially, these virtues were most closely associated with the 'old' *Mittelstand* of small- and medium-sized independents. Much as it was during the nineteenth century, the *Mittelstand* self-image has continued to be marked by a sense of being threatened 'on two fronts'. Fear of social declassment has frequently mobilised *Mittelständler* into interest groups to defend the status quo. From 1948, measures to equalise the burden of war losses (*Lastenausgleich*) for example, prompted much indignant protest. A houseowner wrote: 'I am just another representative of the "owning class" that barely owns enough to be able to live . . . this dual-edged *Lastenausgleich* collars the small, not the large owner.'[83] Pride in independence and a sense of responsibility are frequent motifs in the testimony of those counting themselves part of the middle estate, as is *Niveau*, cultural aspiration. A toy manufacturer, son of a farmer, complemented his commercial success by marrying the daughter of

a highly respected citizen, personally acquainted with Adenauer . . . She's more on the artistic side than I am. I could afford to marry a woman of good family and give her the kind of life she expected . . . Some of [my friends] are entrepreneurs, some are managers, and then there are my friends from the Rotary Club. They come of every occupational group, but the lower limit is very sharply drawn. It's an intellectual group, I can tell you that.[84]

As this quotation also suggests, there are, in the comfortable life-style and social circulation of the upper reaches of the middle estate (sometimes termed the *gehobener* [elevated] *Mittelstand*), points of overlap with the Republic's élites.

Rather as in France, the image of West Germany's civil servants as a grouping of special dignity and destiny, almost an estate within the middle estate, has surrendered little of its traditional currency as a social stereotype. Despite internal grading, with colloquial distinction between Federal railway, post office and police officials (*'kleine Beamten'*) as opposed to administrative and established civil servants proper, and despite the fact that by 1945 the form of the State had changed no less than three times within one civil servant generation, their collective prestige has remained largely intact. Identification with the state and a sense of historical mission—key factors in the civil servants' self-image—evidently form the basis of a typical view of their 'estate' as deserving of an 'appropriate' standard of living and special rights. In 1949, for instance:

The conscientious and exemplary professional civil service has been the fundament of the State for generations! Defend the well-earned rights of civil servants. 'Clear the way for the able!'—this is what we have wanted for a long time. Help your most loyal servants, the suffering civil servants![85]

This awareness of rank was often expressed in early resistance to union organisation, as a union functionary observed:

They may not wear wing-collars to work any more, but their attitudes date from that time. In their eyes, union functionaries are the whipping-boys of the proletariat with whom no common cause can be pursued. They divide everyone into *Beamte und Nicht-Beamte*.[86]

It was also reinforced by rising standards of living and conspicuous wealth in the private sector: by 1957, 94 per cent of a sample surveyed expressed concern about a decline in their collective prestige.[87] More recently, however, an increase in work-to-rule and strike-like action (e.g. 1969, 1974) on the part of officials, together with the undermining of traditional job security (*Berufsverbot* as a possible consequence of the so-called 'Radicals Decree' of 1972) might suggest that the notional '*Beamte*/mere mortals' divide has, to some degree, faded. Again, a higher level of union organisation (overall 77 per cent by 1976) could express a shift of civil servants' focus of identity, on to a more common footing with other 'work-takers'.

Generally, informal sources confirm the tendency reported in survey work at the end of the 1950s and early in the 1960s: that the term *Mittelstand*, favoured particularly by all but the largest independents to denote (what sociologists term) the pre-industrial '*old* middle estate', but used also by medium-level *Angestellte* and *Beamte* to describe their own position in society, is 'most common amongst the groups which the population as a whole agree belong to the social middle'.[88] That their shared values of thrift and diligence were to come to be regarded as a virtual *sine qua non* of membership of West Germany's *Leistungsgesellschaft* is especially apparent in the attempts made, during the Republic's infancy, to cure young workers of what was perceived as 'proletarianisation'.

Locating the precise social position of intellectuals and, in a wider sense, university-trained liberal professionals in the Federal Republic, is problematical. A profusion of labels—which include *die Intellektuellen* (intellectuals), *die Akademiker* (university graduates), *die Intelligenz* (intelligentsia), *die geistigen Arbeiter* (intellectual/brain workers), *die Gebildeten* (the educated)—tends to confuse, rather than clarify an issue which in West Germany has been made all the more sensitive by factors such as the militantly anti-intellectual stance of the National Socialist regime, the role of students and prominent intellectuals during the extra-parliamentary opposition of the late 1960s and in the terrorist and anti-nuclear campaigns of the 1970s and early 1980s. Whilst colloquial reference to *geistige Arbeiter* is suggestive of a basic manual/non-manual distinction whereby the lowly office clerk might be classed together with a

143

university professor,' the weight of the evidence also indicates the existence of a significant divide, cutting across the upper reaches of the white-collar sector, between *Akademiker* and *Nicht-Akademiker*. Association with the historical *Bildungs-bürgertum* appears to have been an important aspect of the *Akademiker* self-image, even under straitened circumstances. In 1948, a refugee lecturer, his life-style 'radically relieved of its "bourgeois" ballast after settling into my tiny, petty-bourgeois quarters', bought a Michaelangelo reproduction with his first allocation of the new Deutsche Mark to prove that:

the '*Bürger* under crossfire' has not died out completely; the assertion that impoverishment and proletarianisation are one and the same is still a Marxist fraud. We are determined, no matter now great our wretchedness, not to become proletarianised, even though—with our torn underwear, our fraying trousers and our split shoes etc.—the external appearance we present is, unfortunately, enough to make even a real old-style proletarian look like a true '*Gent*' [English in original] by comparison.[89]

During the 1950s, academically trained liberal professionals were also given to claiming to be the 'poor cousin' (*Stiefkind*, stepchild) of the entire social order.[90] 'True democracy', remarked a professor in 1960, 'is when every roadsweeper is able to become a professor—provided that he's prepared to put up with the salary', a quip said to have met with 'tremendous mirth' from the audience of economics postgraduates (well capable of knowing that a professorial salary was roughly six times the wages of a sweeper).[91] Overall, the sources suggest continuity in the image of university graduates as a distinct social type, located somewhere above a line dictated in part by the boundaries of what might be termed petty-bourgeois mentality. The distinction is usually clearly preserved, though not always admitted publicly. Ludwig Erhard was asked, for example, in an interview, whether he came from a '*kleinbürgerlich*' family background. 'From a *gutbürgerlich* [solid, middle-class] family background, yes',[92] he replied, with a coyness deemed unnecessary by Franz-Josef Strauss who in 1975 declared: 'I heartily detest provincialism smacking of sauerkraut, for I am intellectual.'[93]

The evidence of informal testimony leaves little doubt that, however confused the nomenclature (for instance: *haute volée*, *crème de la crème, die oberen 10,000, die Geldaristokratie, die Wirtschaftselite, die Prominenz, der Adel* (nobility), *die Schickeria* (the in-crowd), *die Oberklasse, die Reichen, die High Society* etc.) far from being completely levelled or classless, West German society does indeed possess a 'top'.[94] There are signs moreover, that—without doing linguistic violence to the term—the widely-favoured *Oberschicht* might well be interpreted not just in the sociologically rather neutral sense of an 'upper stratum', but also in the sense of an 'upper crust' familiar from the British example. Largely shorn, by the post-war division of Germany, of the old *Junker* aristocratic element whilst at the same time accommodating newer holders of wealth, power or prestige (or all three), West Germany's 'Society' has been reconstituted partly through conscious effort and partly on the basis of tradition. Within a year of capitulation, for example, manuals of social etiquette were demanding that 'one behave decently again' although 'there is no longer a "Society" in the old sense . . . we are unfortunately obliged to live in social chaos', offering examples of behaviour befitting to 'cultivated circles', 'educated people' and 'persons of taste' when attending suppers, receptions, opera premières and international cocktail parties.[95] One manifestation of Society life is membership of the 'correct' club; there is also still a thriving network of local nobility associations, whose central office in Bonn publishes its own journal and updates the *Gotha Handbook*, the highest authority on matters of German lineage. Indeed, available testimony by West German nobles often evinces traces of a feeling of superiority inconsonant with both juridical and material reality. The attitudes within one dispossessed family, as documented by a social worker at the end of the 1940s, were, no doubt, representative of many similar examples:

Ultimately, the one thing which the father did hope to be able to offer his daughters, via his connections, was a good match in marriage. After lengthy efforts, one daughter was settled with X (a gentleman of very appropriate rank) possessing the title which was the very lowest required by the daughter in order to have a proper sign of her station. The children were brought up along these lines, and the family makes no secret of the fact. [The other daughter, working as an *Arbeiterin* on account of the family's financial plight] does not know what to make of the consciousness of her background being instilled into her . . . caught within a conflict of interests, she yearns, on the one hand, to experience the life which her parents, with their tales of the past, depict as befitting her estate (particularly the glittering ball-nights). On the other hand, she wants to be allowed to be like other people, namely her fellow-workers . . .[96]

The notion of a special destiny, dictated by history and by the tradition of *noblesse oblige*, has remained a recurrent motif in the aristocratic self-image;

Above-average character traits and mental capabilities are rare . . . the nobility has always striven to nurture these qualities. In this age of declining authority and of spiritual degeneration, it is the task of the nobility to live out those virtues which are expected of them.[97]

Although the sources suggesting just one fundamental social division between the noble and the bourgeois point to a decline in the class bigotry more typical perhaps of an earlier period, for instance, the Junker joke 'Which animal is most like the human being? Answer: the bourgeois', or the definition of nobles as 'people who do not eat in the kitchen',[98] there are still signs that, even amongst nobles of the younger generation, the distinction is preserved:

Socially, bourgeois girls have very slim chances, unless of course they're rolling in money. So long as they're young and pretty they are sought after, as one has known the noble ones since childhood and is less likely to start relationships with them. But when it comes to marriage, then things are different.[99]

'*Die Geldaristokratie*', the money-aristocracy, is a label which, in colloquial usage, has come to denote not only the noble rich but also those who consolidated or else acquired positions at the helm of big business, forming what is also termed *die Wirtschaftselite*, the economic and industrial élite. The 1950s were of course crucial years in West Germany's economic and social development, and during this period as policies of '*Soziale Partnerschaft*', *Mitbestimmung* and the *Formierte Gesellschaft* were evolving, the question of social class became a matter of some concern in leading entrepreneurial circles. The evidence of their statements indicates a more complex preoccupation with such issues than that exhibited, for example, by the nobility, and accordingly, the images presented are more differentiated. 'Cartels of fear' was Dahrendorf's phrase to characterise Federal German élites; it would seem particularly appropriate to top industrialist and financial circles, whose informal testimony displays a tendency to be, at one and the same time, both defensive and assertive. Thus, whilst typical emphasis of *Leistung* (achievement) as the key to success had a conveniently classless and democratic ring about it, hierarchical assumptions remain typical, as does the emphasis on 'responsibility'. It is possible, therefore, to detect traces of both a rhetorical and a genuine self-image, with the former usually veiling the latter underneath the polite fiction that class does not exist; for instance:

The concept of a capitalistic class society is simply a phantom which clearly is nurtured only to prevent the truth from becoming known. . . . The German entrepreneur, a fundamental and integral element within the social order himself, recognises the basic rights to liberty of every citizen of the State. . . . And, for his part, the entrepreneur is prepared to further the rise of the gifted, to support the acquisition of personal ownership by increasingly broad strata of the people, and to provide active help in the creation of dwellings fit for human habitation.[100]

Tell-tale signs of recognition, behind the hollow rhetoric, of the existence of class distinctions are evident not least in the almost paradoxical manner in which some of this élite's self-made men'—a fine advertisement, one might have thought, for the openness of an 'achievement society'—have tended to play down their humbler origins. A leading businessman during the 1960s commented:

The origins of one's forefathers are a jealously guarded secret in our circles, if one feels that they are not something to be shown. One of our famous industrialists is known to fly into fits of manic rage whenever his father is referred to as a sweetshopkeeper. The same was to be observed recently of a gentleman, newly-risen to the Board of Directors, whose father drove a milk-cart.

This came in response to a survey request, during the early 1960s, for details about the family background of top businessmen. Two-thirds of the sample approached declined to reply. One Board Director reported that his colleagues were 'of the predominant opinion that it is better to say nothing at all on the matter, lest it should become known that membership of a certain stratum does indeed foster one's ascent'.[101] The use, therefore, of rhetoric and secrecy in itself reverberates with sensitivities and assumptions about class; its continuity is indicated, moreover, in the statement, made at the end of the 1970s, by the Republic's foremost consultant for top-bracket personnel:

It is again important today what background [*Haus*] one comes from, for nothing else can replace this kind of socialisation. Of course, these are not the sort of things one cares to mention, out of consideration for the unions and the works' councils.[102]

In drawing together the images conveyed by the informal evidence examined above, two general observations may be made, both of which find some corroboration in the conclusions reached by social scientists who have enquired into the 'pictures of society' held by the West German populace: first, that no one single criterion for class membership appears to obtain, thus typically the number of social groupings identified may vary;[103] secondly, that—somewhat in contrast to British society, for example—there would appear to be less obvious interest in the class origins and characteristics of one's fellows.[104] Nevertheless, a picture emerges of a society divided more or less in accordance with the groupings found in official scources; it remains to be seen whether this picture can be in any way reinforced by evidence taken from representative surveys across society. By synthesising the findings of four separate samples, taken between the 1950s and the early 1970s,[105] it appears that, allowing for marginal overlapping of groups and the combination of stratification criteria, occupation is regarded as the chief determinant of one's position in the social hierarchy. Furthermore, by analysing the frequency and the actual labels given (spontaneously) to the social groupings identified by the respondents, it transpires that:

a. *Arbeiter* (and sometimes *Arbeiterklasse*) is the group named most frequently in occupational models, and the most frequently named group overall (i.e. in mixed models);
b. *Beamte* is, after *Arbeiter*, the second most frequently named group both in occupational models and overall;
c. *Mittelstand* is the most frequently named group in top/middle/bottom

(*Oben/Mitte/Unten*) models, and the third most frequently named group overall;

d. *Angestellte* is the fourth most frequently named group in occupational models and overall;

e. there is less apparent consensus regarding the top of society, with greater variety as to labels, although the 'upper 10,000' and 'the rich' of the earliest survey tended, subsequently, to be replaced, in terms of popularity, by the 'upper stratum' (*Oberschicht*).

Since there would appear to be broad recognition that the wealthiest and most successful constitute a 'top' level of society, there is some justification in modifying the official set of categories slightly by discounting the public relevance of 'assisting family members' and by separating the 'independents' into a 'middle estate' and an 'upper stratum', thereby arriving at the following model: *Arbeiter, Angestellte, Beamte, Mittelstand, Oberschicht*. If this is then collated with the images conveyed in academic and the more detailed informal testimony, the approximate contours of a working class, the middle classes of *Angestellte, Beamte* and the *Mittelstand*, and the upper crust of élites emerge.

The Realities of Class

Having pieced together, from the image material, a broad mapping of West German society—albeit with various uncertainties and ambiguities—one may turn to 'objective' evidence to see how far this mapping is confirmed or needs to be further modified. It is worthwhile noting here the criticism levelled, in 1969, by *Der Spiegel* that 'the Federal Office of Statistics, so painstaking in its annual figures on selected fruit cultivation, cattle slaughter and membership of male-voice choirs, was never allowed to investigate class distinctions within West German society'.[106]

INCOME AND WEALTH
Income statistics indicate certain crude facts on economic existence that are very much at odds with ideologies of classlessness. Allowing for differentiation within the official

occupational categories, the greatest earning homogeneity has, on average, been retained by the self-employed and by civil servants; the differential between *Arbeiter* and *Angestellte* income was not great, but—contrary to what was suggested by the latter's protests against 'levelling'—remained constant, and has also subsequently increased.[107] Starker by far is the imbalance between the incomes of the dependently (waged and salaried) employed, and the independents. Between 1950 and 1970, this annual average per capita income differential actually multiplied tenfold.[108] If in 1950, a self-employed person's household had on average 71 per cent more income at its disposal than a worker's family did, by 1970 the percentage was 116 per cent and 266 per cent by 1978.[109] The fact that the independents have continued to increase their share within the top earnings bracket is even more significant in view of their continuous absolute numerical decline.[110] Graduates' earnings, it may be noted also, are roughly twice those of non-graduates.[111] Clearly, the mass of workers and the majority of salaried employees are not in income groups allowing much capital-intensive acquisition of wealth. Distribution figures for 1950–69 show that a relatively limited number of persons (mainly independents, with some high-earning *Angestellte* and *Beamte*) did disproportionately well during the crucial early 'boom' years, establishing a pattern still prevalent today:[112]

	Proportion of gainfully employed	*Share in expansion of (new) wealth to 1969*
Independents (including farmers)	24.0%	57.0%
Civil servants	4.7%	6.0%
Salaried employees	22.5%	16.0%
Workers	49.2%	12.0%

Moreover, the majority of very rich and powerful commercial concerns today were re-established after the war using *old* (i.e. inherited) wealth. These family concerns include Bosch,

Finck, Haniel, von Opel, Quandt, von Siemens, Stumm, Thyssen, Werhahn and von Oppenheim.[113] By 1966, 74 per cent of the FRG's private wealth was in the hands of just 1.8 per cent of its households.[114] Agricultural assets have become similarly concentrated: between 1949 and 1971, the number of farms fell by 40 per cent, but the overall area of farmland diminished by only 9 per cent, with noble holdings remaining disproportionately large.[115] Many noble families retain considerable assets in both branches, such as Prince Albrecht zu Castell-Castell (2000 hectares of forest, the Castell Bank), the Princes Fürstenberg (20,000 hectares, Fürstenberg Brewery) and the Princes Hohenzollern-Sigmaringen (18,000 hectares, steel mill and plastics factory).[116] Although figures for 1950–78 show that workers, civil servants and (in particular) salaried employees increased their percentual shares in the ownership of private wealth, certain distinctions remain typical: houses are owned most frequently by farmers and other independents; life insurance and bonds by non-agrarian independents, building mortgages by civil servants, and ordinary savings accounts by civil servants, salaried employees and workers.[117] Given the generally small amounts involved in these accounts, it remains unlikely that the average worker or salaried employee could cross the barrier into the kind of economic security enjoyed by the majority of civil servants and independents. Although by 1978, there were roughly 6 million people (some 10 per cent of the population) living on the official poverty line, extreme hardship is a plight determined not solely by class, but by other factors such as age, sex and ethnicity. Race, for instance, has influenced the geography of class: many urban areas of generally low-standard accommodation traditionally associated with the industrial working class— Berlin's Wedding and Kreuzberg, for instance—are now inhabited mainly by *Gastarbeiter*. Equally, thanks to the long-standing tradition of renting by all classes, together with policies of 'mixed' housing and subsidies, the 'two nations' of council tenants and home owners such as are found in Britain are not a phenomenon of the FRG.[118] Settlements for refugees and the homeless do, however, often carry social stigma by their names alone.

POWER

Available data show a fairly even spread, according to paternal occupation, between entrepreneurs, liberal professionals, civil servants and, latterly, salaried employees, characterising the background of top-level politicians as broadly middle-class and not distinctly upper-class to an extent comparable with Britain. Nevertheless, recruitment to high political office in the FRG has followed certain patterns, power mostly falling to those amongst whom—on the basis of existing family tradition (civil servant fathers)[119] or high academic achievement (both, usually—the necessary socialisation and motivation could be expected. The incidence of working-class incumbents of ministerial posts has remained low, although, from 1966, with the Grand Coalition, a number of Social Democrats of working-class parentage moved into ministerial positions. If, in terms of occupational groupings within successive Parliaments, the figures suggest increased participation by the working- and lower-middle classes (with *Arbeiter* and *Angestellte* comprising for the first time, in 1966, the second largest contingent after public servants),[120] one need only examine overall occupational percentages to see a socially imbalanced picture:[121]

Occupational group	% of MPs	% of gainfully employable
Workers	3.0	47.4
Salaried employees	26.4	28.8
Civil servants	27.4	5.5
Independent farmers	7.3	3.3
Other independents	c. 20.0	7.6

Figures for the ninth *Bundestag* (1980–83) show the continuation of this position, with workers accounting for still only 2.3 per cent of its total composition.[122] One might also note that although by the late 1960s there appeared to be only a diminishing correlation between noble lineage and political power, more recently this trend has reversed. In contrast to its size (about 60,000) the nobility has become increasingly overrepresented in Parliament: the tenth *Bundestag* had no less than 13 (nominally, at least), noble Deputies, including four Counts and three Barons.[123]

Within the realm of big business, power has in many instances remained in the hands of those who, under the Kaiser and Hitler, formed a plutocracy, such as the heavy industrial families Thyssen, Krupp, etc. Undoubtedly, the special constellation of circumstances during the early post-war period did permit a number of able men from relatively humble backgrounds to attain positions of power, as managers for instance. According to research on top management, however, the rate of self-recruitment amongst men predominantly from the upper-middle and upper strata has remained high.[124] Nobles are again statistically overrepresented in positions of commercial power (by about 500 times at the top levels of banking).[125] At the formal level, it is largely the interests of a limited number of major (i.e. most powerful) owners and managers, rather than those of small independents that are represented by the Employers' Association, though some constraints on the latter's power (which still includes, for instance, the right to lockout) are present in both the DGB and the legislation on (limited) worker co-determination, as well as the 'property entails social obligation' clause of Republican Basic Law. Rather as in France and the USA, with authority in the FRG being related to function, it is difficult to speak of a distinctive upper-class hegemony. Thanks to the disruptive effect of political events during the twentieth century, there is less obviously a contrast amongst the holders of power in West Germany between 'patricians' and 'meritocrats' than may be found in Britain.[126] The 'meritocrats' are themselves following patrician traditions: academic legal training remains a highly significant requirement for recruitment into the power élite, fulfilling a socialisation function comparable to that of France's *grandes écoles* or Britain's public schools and Oxbridge system. Enke's comment (1974) remains valid: 'Since jurisprudence graduates continue to occupy a central position within the recruitment patterns of several areas (the politically relevant ones especially), one might term the estate of lawyers "The ruling profession".'[127]

EDUCATION AND CONCLUSION

During the troubled late 1960s, the need for educational reforms was an issue of focal importance—a point reflected in the fact that Chancellor Brandt placed it, in 1969, at the head of the list of reform priorities facing the newly-elected socialist-liberal coalition.[128] The interrelationship between education and class in West Germany is one of fundamental importance. With the majority of positions involving the most power, prestige and wealth depending, in an 'achievement society', upon (increasingly higher) academic qualification, the educational process serves as perhaps the single most significant filter of life chances. A determinant of ultimate social class position, it is itself determined by class in terms of continuing inequality of educational opportunity. Census data for 1970 reveal that, of those members of the population with some form of qualification:

77.8% had only a basic school-leaving certificate
8.6% had a middle school leaving certificate
8.2% had a vocational training school certificate
1.0% had an engineering school certificate
1.6% had *Abitur* (conferring right to enter a university)
2.8% had university or teacher training college degree.[129]

What these figures suggest is that even the crude equation of the tripartite schooling system with the broadly three-class structure of society (e.g. *Hauptschule* equals working-class, *Mittel-Realschule* equals middle-class, *Gymnasium*/University equals upper-class) is something of an understatement. Research findings show that, despite partial reforms such as the comprehensive school experiment and the introduction of university grants (BAFöG), 'children's educational level differs only minimally from that of their parents, the parental social position determines that of their offspring'.[130] Dahrendorf's barrier 'dividing an Above from a Below'[131] remains particularly relevant in view of the continuing under-representation of working-class children at all stages of education beyond the *Hauptschule* and, above all, at university:

Students with working-class fathers (in %):[132]

1952/53	4.4
1955/56	5.0
1958/59	5.2
1962/63	5.1
1963	5.9
1967/68	6.7
1973	11.5
1976	13.0
1978	14.8

This disproportionately low percentage must be accounted for not in terms of lack of intelligence, but of class barriers: material (mainly indirect expense of further education);[133] psychological/cultural[134] (linguistic 'codes' being of particular relevance, given the emphasis, within West German assessment modes, on *oral* ability), and administrative (school streaming is both early and inflexible). Just how disadvantaged West German working-class children are with regard to educational opportunity is evident from other comparative statistics: as early as 1961, the percentage of students from a working-class background in Sweden was 14.3 per cent and 25 per cent in the UK. Even in 1971, a worker's child in the FRG had a 0.8 per cent chance of attending university—just one-fifteenth of the chance held by the child of a civil servant.[135] As student financial support becomes increasingly loan- rather than grant-oriented, and with the development of private (so-called élite) universities currently under discussion,[136] the inequality inherent within the educational system—recently recognised to be 'an uninterrupted class- and stratum-specific gap'[137]— seems even more likely to perpetuate ultimate class inequality.

The Federal Republic remains in many respects a divided society although, as we have seen, the various lines of stratification do not always coincide to yield a picture of completely unambiguous classes. A degree of social mobility has taken place, but considerable barriers still exist, disguised perhaps by a high degree of legitimacy or faith in equality of opportunity. In effect, the self-justificatory system of 'pluralist' democracy in the FRG is rather rigid (and certainly not egalitarian) in structure. Without doubt, many traditional factors related to class—such as inherited wealth, the parental role in children's educational achievement, the potential material advantages of noble titles (the buying and selling of which is hardly a matter of simple vanity)[138]—are more important than is actually allowed for by official and public notions of an 'open' *Leistungsgesellschaft*. As regards class awareness, West Germany would appear to be, rather like the USA, less obviously class-ridden than Britain, also sharing similarities with France in the phenomenon of special sectional or 'estate'-consciousness found within a more generalised middle-class awareness. Ultimately, the significance of being working-class in West Germany remains the most unambiguous: workers are generally under-represented in the majority of the good things in life (*Gästarbeiter* even more so); their opportunities for acquiring education, power and wealth are disadvantaged; their jobs are usually the most dangerous, unpleasant and taxing, etc., though tedium may be shared, for example, also by routine white-collar employees. Yet, whilst employment and social security legislation persists in maintaining the formal distinction between *Arbeiter* and *Angestellte*—with its attendant, often discriminatory practices[139]—it seems likely that class awareness will mirror the same division. To date, the sense of psychological and actual social impotence summed up and expressed in the concept of the 'little man' has referred, predominantly, to the working class, some 42 per cent of the gainfully-employed population (plus, of course, their families and those unemployed).

The single most significant social division is thus in many respects that between the workers and the salaried employees, one which divides the working class from the middle classes, the 'little man' from, in effect, the rest of society. So far, the existence of the middle classes would appear to have lent stability to West Germany. With a worsening of the economy, with greater solidarity between workers, *Angestellte* and *Beamte*, the most significant class division could well become one between work-givers and work-takers.

Notes

1. In 1907, for instance, one in every six persons born in East Prussia, Silesia and Pomerania had migrated westwards.
2. A. Crawley, *The Rise of Western Germany* (1973), p. 15.
3. Fifty-three per cent of a sample representative of the general population felt that the prestige of the *Akademiker* would remain constant over the years, Spiegel-Infratest München, *Akademiker in Deutschland* (1980).
4. According to poll figures by the Allensbach Institute, from 27% in 1952, to 45% in 1969, to 49% in 1977. Cf. Table M 15 in M. and S. Greiffenhagen, *Ein schwieriges Vaterland* (1981), p. 340.
5. E.g. Goebbels: 'The *Volk* is an organism, it has *Faust und Stirn*; they are welded into a community by the might of our struggle for existence. . . . Calloused hands and knitted brows change into a stratum of nobility. Hammer and pen belong together', *Der Angriff*, 4 July 1927.
6. Occupational censuses took place in 1882, 1895 and 1907 and, combined with the population census, in 1925, 1933, 1939, 1946 (on an Allied zonal basis); on a Federal basis, in 1950, 1961, 1970. The census scheduled for 1983 was postponed following a ruling by the Federal Constitutional Court. Micro-censuses have also been conducted since 1957.
7. Thus, e.g in 1950 there were 151 economic branches broken down into 74 economic groups, which in turn fell into one of ten economic sections (agriculture, fisheries and forestry; iron/metal production and working; services etc.).
8. *Volkszählung 1961, Schlagwortverzeichnis*, Drucksache No. 7, p. 282; and Merkblatt zur Haushaltsliste, p. 224.
9. *Ibid.*, p. 275.
10. *Volkszählung* (1979), p. 14.
11. Clerics and spokespersons of all other religious communities being classed as *Angestellte*. *Volkszählung 1970*, p. 14.
12. *Ibid.*, p. 14.
13. *Volkszählung 1961*, Drucksache No. 7, p. 270; 1970, p. 14.
14. *Ibid.*
15. *Volkszählung 1950*, Band 31, *Organisation und Technik des Volkszählungswerkes* (publ. 1956), B, p. 49; and *Volkszählung 1961*, Drucksache Nr 7, p. 271; *Ibid.*, and *Volkszählung 1970*, p.14.
16. Although, as the census document apologetically points out: 'for technical reasons, the old term "apprentices" appears on the statistical tables'!, p. 14.
17. Administered by (state-supervised) public law corporations.
18. Cf. the excellent study by H. G. Hockerts, *Sozialpolitische Entscheidungen im Nachkriegsdeutschland: Alliierte und deutsche Sozialversicherungspolitik 1945–1957*, (1980); also 'German Postwar

Social Policies against the Background of the Beveridge Plan. Some Observations Preparatory to a Comparative Analysis', in W. Mommsen (ed.), *The Emergence of the Welfare State in Britain and Germany* (1981).

19. *Angestelltenrentenversicherungsneuregelungsgesetz* of 1957, 9th edn, January 1971, Bundesversicherungsanstalt für Arbeiter, Anhang 18, Anlage 1, pp. 336–9; 2. *Arbeiterrentenversicherungsneuregelungsgesetz* (1957), Anlage 1 (zu Artikel 2, para. 55), Beck'sche edition, pp. 166–8.

20. 9th edition (1971), p. 15.

21. Though the government proposed extending incapacity so as to deem 'reasonable' only those occupations for which the insured person had undergone 'successful' (re-)training within the framework of his-her rehabilitation; in Hockerts, *op. cit.*, p. 360.

22. *Ibid.*, pp. 369–71.

23. In *The Economics of Success* (English edn, 1963), p. 183.

24. Cf. L. Preller, *Praxis und Probleme der Sozialpolitik*, II (1970), pp. 463–4.

25. Prior to the 'Act to Improve the Economic Security of Workers in the Case of Sickness' (1957), they could apply, after waiting three days (*Karenztage*), for benefits amounting to 5 per cent of their basic wage; until 1961, benefit was paid (after two days), together with an employers' subsidy, amounting to 90 per cent of the basic wage, reaching 100 per cent (after one day) in subsequent years.

26. Cf. Industrial Relations Acts, in particular: The Works' Constitution Act (para. 5), the Protection from Dismissal Act (para. 14) and the Labour Courts Act (para. 5).

27. Non-basic periods are scaled according to length of service, the significant distinction being that, for workers, calculation commences at the age of 35, for *Angestellte* at 25 (1972 version). In November 1982, the Federal Constitutional Court judged this regulation to be inconsonant with Article 3 of the Basic Law (1BV 1116/75 and 36/79). Cf. *Die Quelle*, 3/83 pp. 160–61.

28. Cf. entry '*Beamte*' in *Staatslexikon* (Herder Verlag, 1957), esp. pp. 966–70. The confidential 'Report on Allowances for Members of the Federal Public Service', compiled by the Federal Ministry of the Interior, lists 450 special financial perks including, for example, a 'climbing allowance' (3 DM for 20 metres' height, 5 DM for 50, 18 for anything over 300 metres and 25 per cent more in winter)! Cf. 'Die hässlichen Beamten', in *Stern-Magazin*, No. 35, 20 August 1981. In 1977, for example, the Federal Constitutional Court agreed that the standard child allowance was 'inappropriate to their estate' and raised it.

29 And yet there would still appear to be the odium of social stigma/ declassment attached to the institution: even in 1982, according to estimates by the Federal Ministry for Families, only 52 per cent of those entitled actually made use of *Sozialhilfe*. Cf. Neumann and Schaper, *Die Sozialordnung der Bundesrepublik* (1983, 2nd edn), p. 115.

30 Der Minister für Arbeit und Sozialordnung, *Sozialbericht 1980*, pp. 32–3.
31. *Grundgesetz*, Artikel 3 (Gleichheit vor dem Gesetz), 1981 edn, Bundeszentrale für politische Bildung, p. 20.
32. E.g. 1969—workers get six weeks' pay in illness; workers and salaried employees on equal footing for unemployment insurance; introduction of comprehensive schooling experiment; 1970—upper income limit for government savings ('624 Mark') scheme; 1972—self-employed free to join *Angestellte* insurance scheme on voluntary basis.
33. *Bulletin* No. 139, parts II, III, 25 July, 1953.
34. *Für eine Politik der Erneuerung. Regierungserklärung vor dem Deutschen Bundestag vom 13.* October 1982, pp. 51, 38.
35. Cf. Marwick, *Class: Image and Reality in Britain, France and the USA Since 1930* (1980), p. 329.
36. *Ibid.*, p. 256.
37. J. Schumpeter, 'Die sozialen Klassen im ethnisch homogenischen Milieu', *Archiv für Sozialwissenschaft and Sozialpolitik*, Bd 54, 1927.
38. 'Die Bedeutung des Schichtungsbegriffs für die Analyse der gegenwärtigen deutschen Gesellschaft', in *Auf der Suche nach Wirklichkeit* (1979), p. 327.
39. *Ibid.*, p. 328.
40. Research has, however shown distinct qualitative differences between goods purchased by workers and those by others. Similarly, although by 1952, real wages were rising, the *Arbeiter/Angestellte* differential remained fairly constant, whilst that between workers and independents was increasing. Cf. below, section on 'Income and Wealth'.
41. J. Höffner, 'Die Entwicklung im Schicksal und Lebensgefühl der Arbeiterschaft und Wandel der sozialen Leitbilder', in K. Jantz, *et al.*, *Sozialreform und Sozialrecht: Festschrift für Walter Bogs* (1959), p. 160.
42. Professor Dr. W. Röpke, 'Schattenseiten der Teilzahlung', in *Kölnische Rundschau*, No. 7a, 10 January 1954.
43. His italics. Here 'in repetition of my thesis already advanced in 1953', 'Die Bedeutung des Klassenbegriffs', in *Jahrbuch für Sozialwissenschaft*, Bd. 12 (1961), p. 246.
44. Cf. Moore and Kleining, 'Das soziale Selbstbild der Gesellschaftsschichten in Deutschland' in *Kölner Zeitschrift für Soziologie und Sozialpschychologie* (1960), pp. 86–119; E. K. Scheuch, 'Sozialprestige und soziale Schichtung' in *Kölner Zeitschrift etc.* (1961), p. 76; K. Bolte, *Deutsche Gesellschaft im Wandel* (1970), vol. 2; Bolte, Kappe and Neidhardt, *Soziale Ungleichheit* (3rd, rev. edn 1974).
45. 'Social Stratification and Mobility in West Germany', in *The American Journal of Sociology*. 64 (1958–59), p. 9.
46. *Ibid.*, p. 10.
47. See note 15. Indeed, in Kleining's more recent study, the percentage (according to prestige/status mobility) of the *Oberschicht* is put at 0.5

per cent but the separate stratum is retained. Cf. 'Soziale Mobilität in der Bundesrepublik', in *Kölner Zeitschrift etc.*, 27 (1975), p. 273.

48. *Loc. cit.*, p. 112. Cf. Bolte, Kappe and Neidhardt; also Kleining (1975), *loc. cit.*

49. *Gesellschaft und Demokratie in Deutschland* (1968), p. 93.

50. Nor, for that matter, was Moore and Kleining's industrial/non-industrial distinction in the lower-middle and upper-lower strata made by other sociologists, either.

51. Based not on statistical evidence but on the 'not completely illegitimate procedure of . . . informed guesswork', *Gesellschaft und Demokratie in Deutschland*, p. 96. All quotations in this paragraph are taken from this edition, in particular pp. 86–107.

52. Although Deppe reported, in 1963, that a 'thematic shift from factory to office occurred by the mid-50s at the very latest', 'Mitbestimmung und Fremdbestimmung im Bewusstsein der Arbeiter', in *Blätter für deutsche und internationale Politik*, Jg 14, H 3, p. 289.

53. *Das Gesellschaftsbild der Arbeiter* (1961), pp. 216, 245.

54. 'Die soziale Schichtung in der Bundesrepublik' in *Deutsche Rundschau*, Bd 84, No. 10, October 1958, p. 920.

55. *Die Bildungsabstinenz der Arbeiter* (1966), pp. 69 ff., 97 ff.

56. Note how, in his (self-translated) English edition, this is given as 'But on either side of the fence, lack of information and strangeness is easily translated into a feeling of threat', p. 112.

57. 'Gibt es noch ein Arbeiterproletariat?', in *Stimmen der Zeit*, J8 85, Bd 166 (1959/60), p. 161.

58. *Klassenverhältnisse im Spätkapitalismus* (1973), p. 200.

59. *Entwicklung de Klassen- und Sozialstruktur der BRD 1950–1970*, (4 vols, 1973–75).

60. *Materialien zur Klassenstruktur der BRD* (2 vols, 1974), quoted in Claessens, Klonne *et al.*, *Sozialkunde der Bundesrepublik* (1979), p. 300.

61. Tjaden-Steinhauer, *op. cit.*, p. 94; IMSF, *op. cit.*, part 1, p. 153; PKA, *op. cit.*, part 1, p. 269.

62. *Loc. cit.*, p. 925.

63. E.g. Dahrendorf, 'Eine neue deutsche Oberschicht? Notizen über die Eliten der Bundesrepublik', in *Die Neue Gesellschaft*, vol. 9, Jg 1962, H1, pp. 18–31; W. Zapf, in W. Bauer *et al.*, *Beiträge zur Analyse der deutschen Oberschicht* (1964); also *Wandlungen der deutschen Eliten* (1965); H. Pross and K. Boetticher, *Die Manager des Kapitalismus* (1971); E. Enke, *Oberschicht und politisches System* (1974).

64. Bolte/Kappe *et al.*, *Soziale Schichtung*, p. 86.

65. Cf. Pross/Boetticher, *op. cit.*, p. 49: 'The accident of birth remains crucial'; and—cf. Janowitz and Dahrendorf—emphasis is laid on the barriers of educational qualification, itself determined greatly by parental class position.

66. Letter, 11 April 1947, Reuter Papers, DGB-Archiv.

67. 'Unser Beitrag ist nicht gering', *Der Volkswirt* No. 51/52, 24 December 1955.

68. (Frau E. K., allotment-dweller in Krefeld, 'Aus dem Lied des

Arbeiters', 23 March 1962) H. Deist papers, file 40, Fr.-Ebert-Stiftung-Archiv.
69. *Ibid.*
70. Quoted in J. Neven Du Mont (ed.), *After Hitler* (1968), p. 80.
71. Cf. for instance (1971) *Wohnste Sozial, haste die Qual* (1975), pp. 69, 189–90.
72. Popitz, *op. cit.*, p. 204.
73. *Ibid.*, p. 114.
74. Quoted in Grimm, *op. cit.*, p. 99.
75. Quoted in Kern und Schuman, *Industriearbeit und Arbeiterbewusstsein* (1970), p. 240.
76. Quoted in R. Wald, *Industriearbeiter privat* (1967), p. 147.
77. Quoted in G. Wallraff, *Industriereportagen* (1971), p. 103.
78. Conference report 'Der Mensch im Bergbau', No. 5, 1953, file 42/67, Bergbau-Archiv.
79. *Wohnste sozial, loc. cit.*, p. 217.
80. *Ibid.*, p. 13.
81. Quoted in Grimm, *op. cit.*, p. 107.
82. 27 March 1962, Deist Papers, box 40, Fr.-Ebert-Stiftung-Archiv.
83. Letter 26 July 1951, Fette Papers, DGB-Archiv.
84. In Neven Du Mont, *op. cit.*, p. 172.
85. Postcard, 8 January 1949 from Bayrische Beamtenvereinigung to President of Wirtschaftsrat, Frankfurt/Main, Wirtschaftsrat papers, Bestand 2, No. 715, Parlamentsarchiv.
86. In A. Mausolff, *Gewerkschaft und Betriebsrat im Urteil der Arbeitnehmer* (1952).
87. Survey by Deutscher Beamtenbund, in Jostock/Bahrdt *et al.*, *Gibt es noch ein Proletariat?* (1962), p. 81.
88. H. Daheim, 'Die Vorstellungen vom Mittelstand', *Kölner Zeitschrift* etc. (1961), p. 268.
89. Letter, Boehm to A. Wölfers, 1 July 1948, Boehm Papers, Bundesarchiv.
90. Cf. Dr E. Brandl, 'Freie Berufe—Stiefkind des Gesetzgebers?', *Frankfurter Allgemeine Zeitung*, 23 February 1951.
91. Quoted in H. Budde, *Die Arbeitnehmerschaft in der Industriegesellschaft* (1963), p. 85.
92. Quoted in V. Beyme, *Die politische Elite in der Bundesrepublik Deutschland* (1974), p. 40.
93. *Kölner Stadtanzeiger*, 15 February 1975.
94. Cf. survey interviews reported by Moore and Kleining (1958) where the greatest number (113) of spontaneously named symbols to describe the structure of West German society identified a top/middle/bottom; similarly, the greatest number (31.1 per cent) of Daheim's representative sample (1960) mentioned 'die Oberen, die Oberschicht die Oberklasse, die gehobene Schicht, der obere Stand; Pfeil (*Das Gesellschaftsbild der Dreiundzwanzigjährigen*, 1964) reported the particular frequency of 'die oberen 10,000'.
95. Quoted by M. Osterland, 'Benimm-Bücher im Nachkriegs-

deutschland', in *Soziale Welt* (1958), pp. 283–8. Cf. for example, the case where a 'society lady' alleged to have been brawling with a policeman who had charged her with being drunk and disorderly, was let off with a fine. Her lawyer argued that 'after all, it is not as though she is a dockworker drinking away her wages—she was entertaining business clients of her husband's and thus had social obligations'. *Hamburger Echo*, 9 November 1960.

96. Case History 128, in G. Wurzbacher, *Leitbilder gegenwärtigen deutschen Familienlebens 1949–1951* (1969).

97. A. V. Schuckmann, letter to *Epoca* magazine, No. 4 (1964), p. 54.

98. In P. Almqvist, *Eine Klasse für sich—Adel in Deutschland* (1980), p. 25.

99. M. V. Kühlmann, in *ibid.*, p. 193.

100. Bundesvereinigung der deutschen Arbeitgeberverbände, *Gedanken zur sozialen Ordnung der Öffentlichkeit Übergeben.* (March 1953), hectograph, p. 6, file 42/67, Bergbau-Archiv.

101. Quoted in 'Die Clique an der Spitze', *Die Zeit*, 23 December 1966, p. 32.

102. In Almqvist, *op. cit.*, p. 27.

103. Cf. the stratum-determinant variations (income/prestige/occupation) reported by R. Mayntz, *Soziale Schichtung und Sozialer Wandel in einer Industriegemeinde* (1958), pp. 98 ff; Daheim, *op. cit.*, pp. 242–3; Moore and Kleining, *op. cit.*, p. 367; K. Mayer, 'Soziale Mobilität und die Wahrnehmung gesellschaftlicher Ungleichheit', in *Zeitschrift für Soziologie*, J81, H2, April 1972, pp. 156, 173.

104. Reflected in, e.g. the findings by Moore and Kleining that interviewees gradually increased the number of strata perceived the longer they were questioned (pp. 364 f.), and by Mayer that 'for the majority of interviewees, naming social differentiations was clearly an unfamiliar task' (p. 163), leaving aside the instances where respondents were completely unable to give a reply.

105. Moore and Kleining, 'Das Bild etc.' (1959); H. Daheim, 'Die Vorstellungen etc.' (1960); W. Schusser, *Ein empirischer Beitrag zur Diskussion um die Abgrenzung von Arbeitern und Angestellten*, Dissertation (Erlangen, 1970); K. Mayer, 'Soziale Mobilität etc.', (1972), Pages (a) 354–75 (b) 236–77 (c) 352–60 (d) 156–76.

106. 28 July 1969, quoted in Claessens *et al.*, *op. cit.*, p. 224.

107. Official figures for *Angestellte* salaries are not available prior to 1957. J. Krejci, *Social Structure in Divided Germany* (1976), pp. 90–3; B. Schäfers, *Sozialstruktur und Wandel der Bundesrepublik Deutschland* (1979), p. 66, Cf. also S. Hradil, *Soziale Schichtung in der Bundesrepublik* (1977), p. 28.

108. IMSF, *op. cit.*, pp. 67–8.

109. Wallner/Funke-Schmitt-Rink, *Soziale Schichtung und soziale Mobilität* (1980), p. 43; 'Income justice still a long way off', *DGB-Report* 18/1980, p. 2.

110. In 1950, there were 3,245,000 'independents' (14.5 per cent of the gainfully employed population), with 3,168,000 'assisting family members' (13.8 per cent). By 1976, these figures were 2,402,000 (9.1

per cent) and 1,250,000 (4.6 per cent) respectively. Bundesminister für Arbeit und Sozialordnung (Hrsg.), *Statistisches Taschenbuch 1983*, section 2.5; Schäfers, *op. cit.*, p. 178.

111. According to a Spiegel/Infratest survey in 1980, graduates earned 4900 DM gross monthly, others only 1800 (on average), with 65 per cent of all gainfully employed receiving less than 2000 DM net, but just 13 per cent of graduates. *Akademiker in Deutschland* (1980).

112. Claessens *et al.*, *op. cit.*, p. 226.

113. B. Engelmann, *Das Reich zerfiel—die Reichen blieben* (1972); Wallraff and Engelmann. *Ihr da oben—wir da unten* (1981), pp. 202–3, for these and other examples.

114. Hradil, *op. cit.*, p. 32; Cf. also Krejci, *op. cit.*, p. 53.

115. Krejci, *ibid.* Top of the list is Prince Johannes Thurn und Taxis who with 34,000 hectares is the largest private landowner in Europe.

116. See note 113.

117. Presse und Informationsamt der Bundesregierung (Hrsg), *Gesellschaftliche Daten 1982* (1982), pp. 176–7.

118. Owner-occupation is currently about 33 per cent, most frequent amongst the self-employed.

119. Cf. W. Zapf, 'Wandlungen der deutschen Elite', *loc. cit.*, pp. 17 ff.

120. Yet note, for example, that even in the industrial '*Arbeiterstadt*' Mannheim, three of the four SPD and CDU parliamentary candidates in 1969 were professors, prompting the comment (from the local SPD secretary): 'Maybe in the 70s we'll finally have a man from the worker-estate again'. *Der Spiegel*, No. 39 (1969), p. 46.

121. K. V. Beyme, *op. cit.*, p. 52. Cf M. Kruk's figures on the big business lobby within the Bundestag during the mid-1960s (1:5 MPs being involved in business at managerial level): *Die oberen 30,000* (1967), esp., pp. 101–6.

122. *Bundestag* 1980–83: (in %)
　33.3 Civil servants
　　6.6 Salaried employees in public service
　　6.9 Holders of government office
　12.1 Salaried employees in political and social organisations
　10.6 Salaried employees in commerce
　14.1 Independents
　12.1 Liberal professionals
　　2.3 Workers
　　1.5 Housevives
Fischer Weltalmanach 1983.

123. In 1965, there were 10. Cf. v. Beyme, *op. cit*, p. 41.

124. Cf. Pross and Boetticher, *op. cit.*; Baumanns and Grossman, *Die deformierte Gesellschaft* (1969); Zapf, 'Sozialprofil westdeutscher Führungsgruppen', in *Studien und Berichte* 3 (1964) pp. 14–15; M. Jungblut, 'Die Clique an der Spitze', in *Die Zeit*, 23 December 1966, p. 32.

125. According to 1979 figures given by Almqvist, *op. cit.*, p. 11. Kruk (*op. cit.*) calculated that, of 10,000 'ordinary citizens', five held top

commercial positions, whereas of the same number of nobles, there were 138, p. 120. See also the list of positions held by nobles, pp. 124–32.

126. Cf. Marwick, *op. cit.*, pp. 343–3.
127. *Oberschicht und politisches System der Bundesrepublik* (1974), pp. 144–5. Marriage, according to a survey, does not help much: 'Does it pay to marry the boss's daughter? Only if one loves her, say the sociologists. It is immaterial to one's career. They have established that a worker's son who makes "a good match" will take just as long to reach a managerial position as he would if he married the daughter of another worker', 'Wie wird man Generaldirektor?', *Frankfurter Rundschau*, 27 August 1964.
128. Government declaration of 1969.
129. Statistisches Bundesamt, *Bevölkerung und Kultur, Volkszählung 1970*, H 3, p. 22.
130. Altendorf/Baecker *et al.*, *Arbeiterkinder an den Hochschulen* (1978), p. 11.
131. See the section on 'Academic Images'.
132. Wallner and Funke-Schmitt-Rink, *op. cit.*, p. 27.
133. With university fees not uniformly abolished until 1972. Similarly, a governmental enquiry in 1975 revealed, for example, that in only 33 per cent of unskilled labourers' families (but in 76 per cent of self-employed) did each child have a bedroom of its own (in which it could do homework, etc). *Bericht der Sachverständigenkommission Familie und Sozialisation, 2 Familienbericht* (1975), Bundesministerium für Jugend, Familie und Gesundheit, p. 20.
134. Cf. Grimm, *op. cit.*, also Hradil, *op. cit.*, pp. 46–51.
135. H. Peisert, *Soziale Lage und Bildungschancen in Deutschland* (1967), p. 67, quoted in Hradil, *op. cit.*, p. 48. Wallner and Rink, *op. cit.*, p. 27.
136. Cf. B. Engholm, 'Der diskrete Charme der Elite', in *Der Spiegel*, No. 8, 20 February 1984, pp. 46–7.
137. Altendorf and Baecker *et al.*, *op. cit.*, p. 11.
138. Note, for instance, the comment in the *Deutsches Adelsarchiv*: 'Who would have imagined that, in postwar years, mere possession of noble titles would be so well-received amongst creditors? The Baron, the Count and the Prince clearly still enjoy such widespread trust that it became terribly easy for name-swindlers and con-men to pursue their wicked trade', 1963/64, pp. 6–7.
139. E.g. separate toilets, those for workers being marked 'Men/Women' with no locks; those for salaried employees 'Ladies/Gentlemen', with lockable doors, etc. Cf. Wallraff and von der Grün, *Unsere Fabrik* (1979), p. 19.

CHAPTER FIVE

Conclusion: The Significance of Class

Perhaps the essential characteristic of true scholarship is that it invites a dialogue between author and reader. But all readers, I hope, will have been persuaded of the crucial and continuing significance of social distinctions in a wide range of societies and further, will have come to appreciate the value and uses of the pragmatic historical approach outlined in the Introduction.

The first substantive chapter of this book (on the upper class) refused to take as given the hypothesis that in twentieth-century society there is a capitalist or bourgeois class, and sought the nature of the upper class in the different histories of the three countries studied, arguing, however, that the widely-held view that the British upper class is somehow highly exceptional is not really accurate. The contention was that there is overwhelming evidence to indicate that a certain aggregate of individuals do exercise, *if they care to avail themselves of the opportunity,* disproportionate power and, quite certainly, enjoy highly disproportionate access to the good things of life. The attempt was made to resolve some of the difficulties in the existing literature where there is said to be a very tiny ruling class, or élite, operating through a separate and larger governing class, by suggesting that the reality is actually of an extended upper class which, while containing within it different fractions, takes its characteristic tone from the most long-established and prestigious elements at its centre.

The American case offers most difficulties, and also more signs of change over the period studied. Until the Second World War at least, there was a strong 'provincialism' in American society which meant that many parts of that geographically sprawling nation had no recognisable upper

165

class. There is a link here with Chapter 3 where it is shown that some of the genuine reality of the Czech notion of themselves as a nation of 'little people' was due to the separation of the Czech Lands from the great central European metropolitan capital of Vienna, which made Czechoslovakia distinctively provincial in character. Compared with Britain, France, America (and Germany) in the inter-war years, Czechoslovakia was far from a fully developed industrial nation: hence, rather than one extended upper class there appears to be two separate, rather inchoate classes. But whatever the difficulties in respect to the top-most class, this chapter brings out very clearly the way in which social distinctions established in an earlier period persist whatever the democratic rhetoric of a government born out of a rejection of the autocratic and semi-feudal traditions of the Austro-Hungarian empire. In the developed, self-conscious societies of Britain, France and America a wealth of testimony, both witting and unwitting, about class distinctions can be drawn from literature, both popular and canonised. On the whole, Czech novels are less helpful, though Chapter 3 does show some of the ways in which widely accepted assumptions about the nature of social distinctions are represented in novels.

There are parallels to be drawn between West Germany at the end of the Second World War and the new Czechoslovak Republic at the end of the First World War. Chapter 4 brings out clearly once more that political ideologies are not usually effective in overcoming historical legacies. The clearest framework of class in the Federal Republic, indeed, is shown to be the long-established table of professional and occupational distinctions, linked directly to the distinctions of treatment enshrined in social legislation (this is directly paralleled in Czechoslovakia and, indeed, in the Britain of the inter-war years).[1] For all the political rhetoric and deliberate Americanisation, a distinctive and class-aware working class quite evidently continued to exist through the economic miracle and into Germany's affluent society. There is less clarity at the top, but evidence of many of the elements identified in Chapter 2; however the notion of an extended upper class (most applicable in Britain and France, less so in America) clearly has little relevance, partly no doubt because of the sharp discontinuities of German history.

Conclusion: The Significance of Class

These essays are cumulative. Their strength is that they are drawn directly from evidence: novels, films, and all of the immense variety of sources which historians can draw upon. Too many books on class are simply refinements and analyses of other books on class; thus do books beget books, getting further and further away from the most concrete evidence there is, the actual products of the societies studied. What comes out strongly and unambiguously is that class, however defined in detail, continues to be of the utmost importance in contemporary society. Class may be a 'contested' concept, as Peter Calvert maintains,[2] but that does not mean, as he goes on to insist, that it should be abandoned, only that it must be examined with the greatest care, and without too many preconceptions.

Notes

1. Arthur Marwick, *Class: Image and Reality in Britain, France and the USA since 1930* (1980), pp. 62–71.
2. Peter Calvert, *The Concept of Class: An Historical Study* (1982), p. 152.

Select General Bibliography

This Select Bibliography is confined to major, and mainly recent, works, which can themselves be used as guides to the enormous literature. Bibliographical information for the specialist topics of the individual chapters can be derived from the notes to these chapters.

Abrams, Philip, *Historical Sociology* (1982).

Almond, Gabriel A. and Verba, Sidney, *The Civic Culture: Political Attitudes and Democracy in Five Nations* (1963).

Althusser, Louis, *For Marx* (1969).

Ardagh, John, *The New France* (1970).

Atkinson, A.B., *The Economics of Inequality* (1975).

Atkinson, R.E., *Knowledge and Explanation in History* (1978).

Badcock, C.R., *Lévi-Strauss: Structuralism and Sociological Theory* (1975).

Barthes, Roland, *The Empire of Signs* (1970, English translation 1983).

Bédarida, François, *A Social History of England 1851–1975* (1979).

Bellon, Bertrand, *Le Pouvoir financier et l'industrie en France* (1980).

Bence-Jones, Mark and Montgomery-Massingherd, Hugh, *The British Aristocracy* (1979).

Bendix, R. and Lipset, S.M., *Class, Status and Power* (1966).

Benson, Leslie, *Proletarians and Parties* (1978).

Benwell Community Project, *The Making of a Ruling Class* (1978).

Birnbaum, Pierre *et al.*, *La Classe dirigeante française* (1978).

Blackburn, R., *Ideology in Social Science* (1972).

Blondel, John, *Contemporary France: Politics, Society and Institutions* (1974).

Bowley, A.L., *Wages and Income in the United Kingdom since 1860* (1937).

Briggs, Asa, 'The Language of Class in the Early Nineteenth

Select General Bibliography

Century', in A. Briggs and J. Saville (eds.) *Essays in Labour History* (1960).

Bulmer, Martin (ed.) *Working-Class Images of Society* (1975).

Burgess, Keith, *The Challenge of Labour* (1980).

Burnham, James, *The Managerial Revolution* (1940).

Calvert, Peter, *The Concept of Class: An Historical Introduction* (1982).

Carr-Saunders, A.M. and Jones, D. Caradog, *A Survey of the Social Structure of England and Wales* (1927).

Centers, Richard, *The Psychology of Social Classes* (1949).

Clarke, John, Critcher Chas and Johnson, Richard (eds.), *Working-Class Culture: Studies in History and Theory* (1979).

Coleman, Richard P. and Rainwater, Lee, *Social Standing in America: New Dimensions of Class* (1978).

Crawley, A., *The Rise of Western Germany* (1973).

Cronin, James, *Industrial Conflict in Modern Britain* (1979).

Cronin, James and Schneer, Jonathan, *Social Conflict and the Political Order in Modern Britain* (1982).

Crouch, Colin, *Class Conflict and the Industrial Relations Crisis* (1977).

Dahrendorf, Ralf, *Class and Class Conflict in Industrial Society* (1959).

Dahrendorf, Ralf, *Conflict after Class* (1967).

Dahrendorf, Ralf, *Society and Democracy in Germany* (1967).

De Negroni, François, *La France Noble* (1974).

Dickson, Tony (ed.), *Scottish Capitalism* (1980).

Dogan, M., *L'Origine sociale de personnel parlementaire français* (1965).

Domhoff, G. William, *Who Rules America Now?* (1983).

Dupeux, Georges, *French Society 1789–1970* (1972).

Durkheim, Emile, *The Division of Labour in Society* (1st French edition 1893, English translation 1933).

Elton, Geoffrey, *The Practice of History* (1967).

Erickson, Charlotte, *British Industrialists: Steel and Hosiery 1850–1950* (1959).

Ferré, Louise-Marie, *Les Classes sociales dans la France contemporaine* (1934).

Fidler, John, *The British Business Élite: Its Attitudes to Class, Status and Power* (1981).

Florence, P. Sargent, *Ownership, Control and Success of Large Companies* (1961).

Furbank, P.N., *Unholy Pleasure: the Idea of Social Class* (1985).

Gallie, Duncan, *Social Inequality and Class Radicalism in France and Britain* (1983).

Gardiner, Patrick, *The Nature of Historical Explanation* (1952).

Gathorne-Hardy, Jonathan, *The Public School Phenomenon* (1977).

Giddens, Anthony, *The Class Structure of the Advanced Societies* (new edition, 1980).

Giddens, Anthony and Hale, David (eds.), *Classes, Power and Conflict* (1982).

Glass, D.V. (ed.) *Social Mobility in Britain* (1954).

Goldthorpe, J.H. *et al.*, *Social Mobility and Class Structure in Modern Britain* (1980).

Gottschalk, Louis (ed.), *Generalisation and the Writing of History* (1963).

Habermas, Jürgen, *Communicaton and the Evolution of Society* (English translation 1979).

Hajda, Jan (ed.), *A Study of Contemporary Czechoslovakia* (1955).

Halbwachs, Maurice, *Les Classes sociales* (1942).

Halbwachs, Maurice, *The Psychology of Social Class* (1959).

Hall, Stuart (ed.), *Culture, Media and Language* (1980).

Halsey, A.H. *et al.*, *Origins and Destinations* (1980).

Heath, A.C., *Social Mobility* (1982).

Hunt, Pauline, *Gender and Class Consciousness* (1980).

Ingham, John N., *The Iron Barons: A Social Analysis of the American Urban Élite* (1978).

Jeanneney, Jean-Noël, *François de Wendel en république: l'argent et le pouvoir 1914–1940* (1975).

Jeffries, Vincent and Ransford, H. Edward, *Social Stratification: A Multiple Hierarchy Approach* (1980).

Jordan, Z. A. (ed.), *Karl Marx: Economy, Class and Social Revolution* (1971).

Keller, Suzanne, *Beyond the Ruling Class: Strategic Élites of Modern Society* (1963).

Kendall, Walter, *The Revolutionary Movement in Britain, 1900–1921* (1969).

Kolko, Gabriel, *Wealth and Power in America* (1962).

Krejci, J., *Social Structure in Divided Germany* (1976).

Laroque, Pierre, *Les Grandes problèmes sociaux contemporains* (1954–55).

Laroque, Pierre, *Les Classes sociales* (1972).

Lhomme, Jean, *Le Problème des classes* (1938).

Lukács, Georg, *History and Class Consciousness* (new German edition 1967, English translation 1971).

Mamatey, Victor S. and Luza, Radomir, *A History of the Czechoslovak Republic, 1918–1948* (1973).

Marceau, Jane, *Class and Status in France* (1977).

Marwick, Arthur, *Class: Image and Reality in Britain, France and the USA since 1930* (1980).

Marwick, Arthur, *The Nature of History* (revised edition 1981).

McLennan, Gregor, 'History and Theory: Contemporary debates

and directions', in *Literature and History,* vol. 10, no. 2 (1984), pp. 139–64.

Mommsen, W. (ed.), *The Emergence of the Welfare State in Britain and Germany* (1981).

Neale, R.S., *Class in English History 1680–1850* (1981).

Neale, R.S., *History and Class: Essential Readings in Theory and Interpretation* (1983).

Newcomer, Mabel, *The Big Business Executive* (1965).

O'Conner, John E. and Jackson, Martin, *American History: American Films* (1979).

Olivova, Vera, *The Doomed Democracy, Czechoslovakia in a Disrupted Europe* (1972).

Ossowski, Stanislaw, *Class Structure in the Social Consciousness* (1963).

Parkin, Frank, *Marxism and Class Theory: A Bourgeois Critique* (1979).

Perelman, Selig, *A Theory of the Labor Movement* (1928).

Perkin, Harold, *The Origins of Modern English Society* (1969).

Pessen, Edward, 'Social Structure and Politics in American History', *American Historical Review,* vol. 87. no. 5 (1982).

Poulantzas, Nicos, *Political Power and Social Classes* (first French edition 1970, English translation, 1973).

Reid, Ivan, *Social Class Differences in Britain* (1977).

Robertson, David, *Class and the British Electorate* (1984).

Rosshides, Daniel W., *The American Class System* (1976).

Rubinstein, W.D. (ed.), *Wealth and the Wealthy in the Modern World* (1980).

Scott, John, *The Upper Classes: Property and Privilege in Britain* (1982).

Sennat, Julius, *Habermas and Marxism* (1979).

Simiand, François, *Cours d'economie politique* (1929).

Sontag, Susan (ed.), *A Barthes Reader* (1982).

Stanworth, P. and Giddens, A, *Élites and Power in British Society* (1974).

Suleiman, Ezra N., *Élites in French Society* (1978).

Thompson, E.P., *The Poverty of Theory* (1978).

Thompson, F.M.L., *English Landed Society in the Nineteenth Century* (1963).

Warner, W. Lloyd, *Social Class in America: the Evaluation of Status* (1960).

Warner, W. Lloyd and Ableggan, James, *Big Business Leaders in America* (1963).

Westergaard, J. and Ressler, H, *Class in a Capitalist Society: a Study of Contemporary Britain* (1975).

Willener, Alfred, *Images de la société et classes sociales* (1957).
Winter, Jay (ed.), *The Working Class in Modern British History: Essays in Honour of Henry Pelling* (1983).
Wright, Erik Olin, *Class, Crisis, and the State* (1978).

Index

Index